Richard Scarry's
Best Rainy Day Book Ever

Random House
New York

Huckle and Pig Will are coloring pictures and hanging them on the wall. Some they color with crayons and some with Magic Markers or water colors. As you go through this book, you will find that all the workers in Busy Town are making things right out of this book. You can make them, too, if you just follow the simple directions. All you need are some colors, a pair of scissors, and paste.

Someone is spilling paint all over the main street of Busy Town. Who can it be? "Stop that driver!" shouts Sergeant Murphy as he jumps on his motorcycle.

At the fire department, busy painters are painting the fire engine a bright red. They can't be the ones who have made the mess on the road. They were careful to put down papers before painting.

Harry Bear is cutting out a valentine.
His twin brother, Charlie, has already
made one and is giving it to Sally Bear.
It is fun to make your own valentines
and give them to people you love.

Peter is making a toy car.
He cuts out the drawing and
then pastes it together.
That's a very nice car you
have, Peter!

At the school the painters are painting the school bus orange. Their helpers are mixing red and yellow paint. Red and yellow make orange.

Oh-oh! Now Sergeant Murphy can see who is making the mess on the road. It is Mr. Paint Pig, who is delivering paints to the workers in Busy Town. He doesn't know that the tops have come off the cans and paint is flying all over the road.

"Please stop, Mr. Paint Pig!" shouts Sergeant Murphy.

Joseph and Josephine have taken the tick-tack-toe sheet out of the book and they are playing the game together. Who do you suppose has won the most times?

Detectives Sam and Dudley are making paper dolls of themselves. They have cut out different costumes for the dolls to wear as disguises.

Mr. PAINT PIG

Kathleen Kitty has made a mobile. She and her friend Mabel watch it turn slowly in the breeze.

Billy Bunny is mailing to a sick friend a get-well card that he made. Isn't that nice?

Bananas Gorilla is giving his Bananamobile a fresh coat of yellow paint.

Be careful you don't paint your bananas, Bananas! Painted bananas are not good for you.

And look! There is Lowly Worm cleaning up Mr. Paint Pig's mess with his street cleaner.

What are Robert and Rosie drawing? They won't know until they finish connecting the dots.

Harry is making a toy train. He has made an engine and a train car. He is now pasting together another train car. How long will it be?

6

The children have made a Pin-the-Tail-on-the-Donkey game from the book. So far nobody has been able to pin the tail in the right place.

Do you think Bobby Raccoon will pin his closer to the "X"?

Mr. PAINT PIG

Little Louie blows his whistle just like Sergeant Murphy, but still Mr. Paint Pig doesn't stop.

DECEMBER

Freddie and Florence are making a calendar. They write in the numbers themselves and then circle the important days like birthdays, Christmas, and other holidays.

When is your birthday?

Farmer Alfalfa is painting his tractor green.
He is also painting his smock green.
His helpers are mixing blue and yellow paint to
make green.

Willy made a paper plane.
Zoom! Look at it fly!

Flossie cuts out and colors
her own bookplates. Then she
pastes them in her books so that
everyone will know the books
belong to her.

Alberta has made an Easter
bunny with chicks and eggs
for an Easter decoration.

Agnes gives her mother
a card for Mother's Day.
She made it herself!
My, wasn't her mother pleased!

Walter Mouse, driving his crayon car,
shouts to Mr. Paint Pig to stop.
But Mr. Paint Pig doesn't hear him.

Georgie Pig hangs up the string
of flags he has colored in the book.
See them flutter in the wind.

Sailor Bill and his friends
are painting his boat blue.
Don't fall off, Sailor Bill.

Jimmy Fox is
building houses which
he has cut out
of this book.

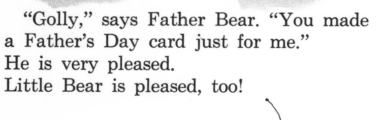

"Golly," says Father Bear. "You made
a Father's Day card just for me."
He is very pleased.
Little Bear is pleased, too!

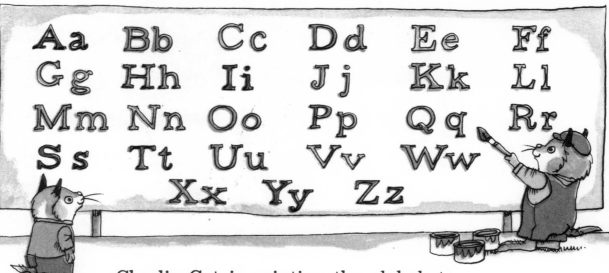

Aa Bb Cc Dd Ee Ff
Gg Hh Ii Jj Kk Ll
Mm Nn Oo Pp Qq Rr
Ss Tt Uu Vv Ww
Xx Yy Zz

Charlie Cat is painting the alphabet
all different kinds of colors.

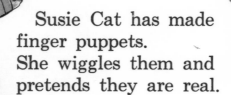

Susie Cat has made
finger puppets.
She wiggles them and
pretends they are real.

Elmer Rabbit makes
Easter cards to give
to his friends
at Eastertime.

HAPPY EASTER

"Stop!"
"Stop!"
"Stop!" shout three funny birds.
But Mr. Paint Pig does not stop.

Mr. PAINT PIG

Sidney and Sandra are painting their airplane violet.
Their helpers are mixing red and blue paint to make violet.

Betty has made birthday
place cards for her
birthday party.

Look at the Halloween witch
Henry has made to put in his window.
Where are you flying to, old witch?

Look out, Sergeant Murphy!
Wet paint is slippery.
You *must* get Mr. Paint Pig
to stop, Sergeant Murphy!

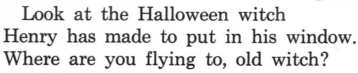

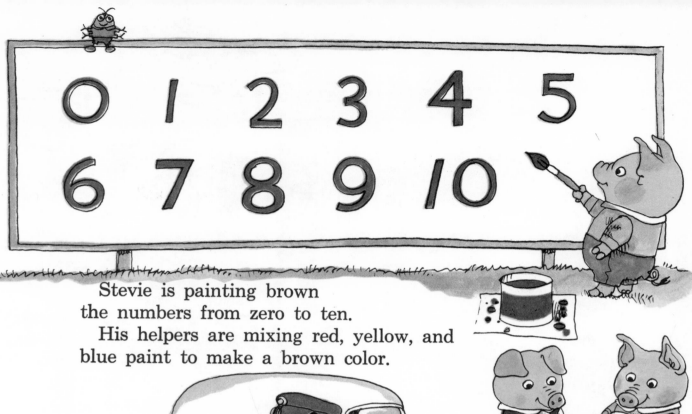

0 1 2 3 4 5
6 7 8 9 10

Stevie is painting brown
the numbers from zero to ten.
His helpers are mixing red, yellow, and
blue paint to make a brown color.

Reddy Fox received a present from his grandmother.
To thank her, he made a thank-you card.
He is giving it to the mailman to deliver.

See the felt-tip marker car.

Mr.
PAINT
PIG

The painters are painting
the passenger car pink and white.
Red and white make pink.

Albert has used the book
to make Christmas decorations.
He hangs them on his
Christmas tree.

Joan makes a Thanksgiving
turkey to stick up on her window.

Georgie is painting
the tank car gray.
White and black make gray.

The engineer is painting
his engine black.
He likes red wheels, though.

Harold made a birthday card
to go on Carol's present.

Mr. PAINT PIG

Sergeant Murphy is catching up now.
Keep after him, Sergeant Murphy!

Well!!! Sergeant Murphy finally stopped Mr. Paint Pig, who was shocked to see what he had done. He promised that in the future he would always keep the tops of his paint cans on tightly.
He promised never to make such a mess again . . . and he thanked Lowly for cleaning up after him.

Now . . . when YOU color and paste, DON'T make a mess like Mr. Paint Pig.
But, of course, you wouldn't do that, would you?

Follow
all directions!

Mr.
PAINT
PIG

All the animals are ready to start coloring in this book.
Are you ready, too? You can begin by coloring this page.
On your mark . . . get set . . . GO!

TAPE

How To Use

Happy Birthday Mommy

This Book

You can color these pages with different things . . . crayons, colored pencils, most felt-tip pens, chalks, water colors. The paper is heavy enough to take color on both sides.

The ink of some felt-tip pens will go through to the other side of the page. Make sure you have the right kind of pen! Test your pen by coloring the pencil cup on the opposite page. Did the color go through the paper?

Water colors will make the paper buckle a bit. If you want to keep the paper flat, first tear out your page and tape all 4 sides to heavy cardboard or a drawing board. Masking tape works best. Let your painting dry thoroughly before you take off the tape. On a rainy day, you may have to let your painting dry overnight.

Some pages in this book call for scissors, paste or sticky tape, and other materials besides colors. The directions on these pages will tell you just what you need.

You may find it easier to work on a page if you tear it out first. Here's how to tear without ripping. Fold the page back and forth several times along the perforated line (the line of little punched-out holes). Then hold down the inside margin with one hand and tear gently along the perforated line with the other hand. Out comes the page!

Here are some of the special things you can make and do in this book:

And of course there are lots and lots of pages just to color – hard pages and easy pages. Have fun!

MAKING A CALENDAR

Let's start making a calendar.

There are 12 months in a year. Some months have 30 days and some have 31. February has only 28 days (except in Leap Year, when it has 29). Each calendar page in this book will tell you how many days the month has.

You will want to fill in the numbers for the days of each month. First you must know on which day of the week the month starts. Look at a printed calendar or ask your mother or father to tell you.

Once you know what day a month begins on, write a "1" in the correct square at the top of the calendar page. Then fill in the rest of the numbers for the month. Write the numbers from left to right on each line, just as Huckle has done below.

In some months there may not be enough squares for all the numbers. In that case, the last number or two will have to share a square at the bottom of the calendar. See how Huckle's 31st day is sharing a square?

On Sundays and special holidays you can circle the numbers in red or write them in a different color. Be sure to circle your own birthday!

After you write in all the numbers, color the pictures on the calendar page. Then hang it up in your room.

Now you can start making YOUR calendar. January is on the next page. You will find the rest of the months farther back in the book.

JANUARY						
SUNDAY	MONDAY	TUESDAY	WEDNESDAY	THURSDAY	FRIDAY	SATURDAY
					1	2
③	4	5	6	7	8	9
⑩	11	12	13	14	15	16
⑰	18	19	20	21	22	23
24/㉛	25	26	27	28	29	30

31 DAYS	JANUARY			NEW YEAR'S DAY—JAN. 1		
SUNDAY	MONDAY	TUESDAY	WEDNESDAY	THURSDAY	FRIDAY	SATURDAY
			1	2	3	4
5	6	7	8	9	10	11
12	13	14	15	16	17	18
19	20	21	23	24	25	26
27	28	29	30	31		

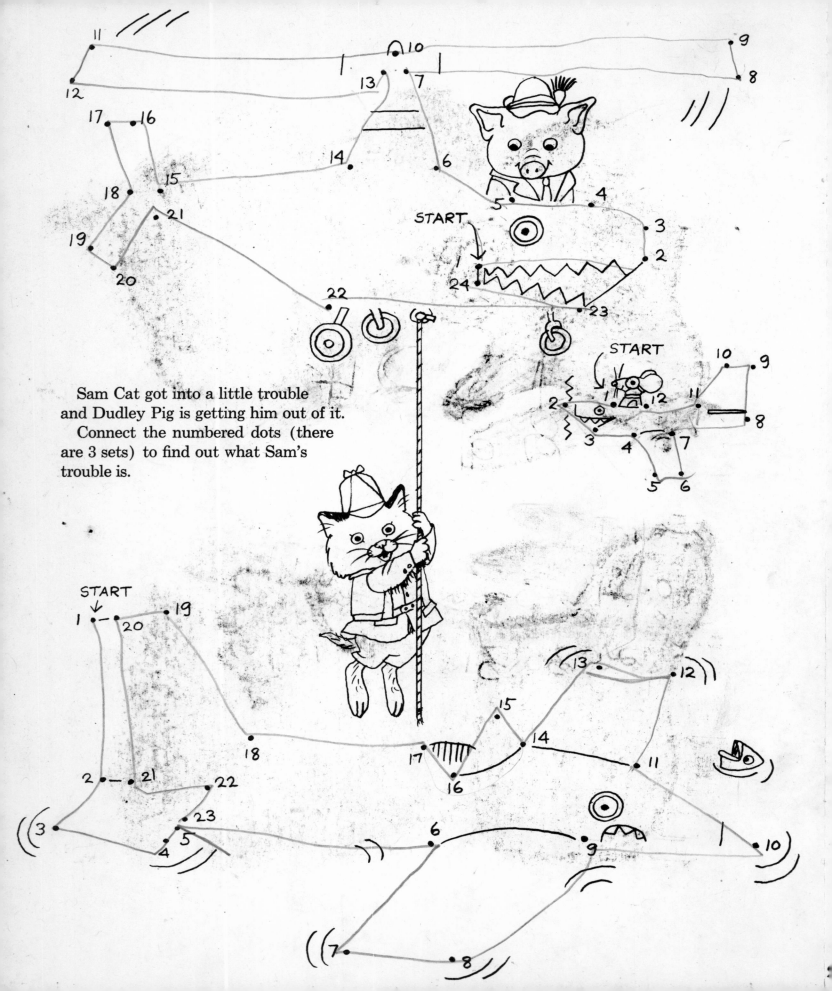

Sam Cat got into a little trouble
and Dudley Pig is getting him out of it.
Connect the numbered dots (there
are 3 sets) to find out what Sam's
trouble is.

START

START

START

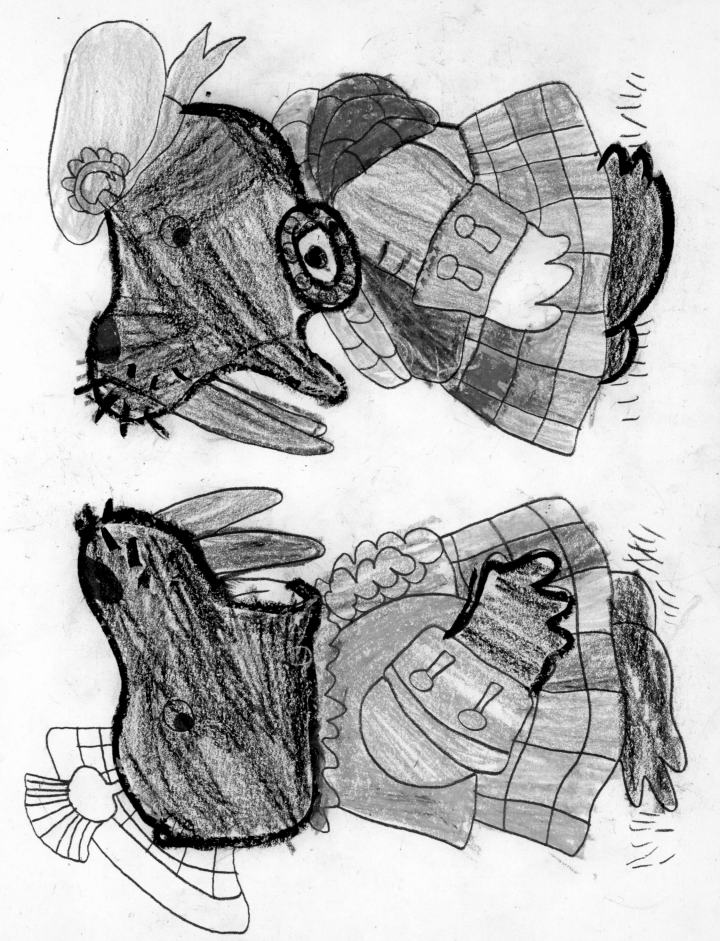

Rory and Angus MacWalrus

COLOR MIXING

Kathleen Kitty is going to mix her own colors. Can you mix yours?

Color the worm all over with red, then with yellow—and it will come out orange.

Yellow and blue will give you a green frog.

Now try mixing the colors listed on the other pictures. What do you get?

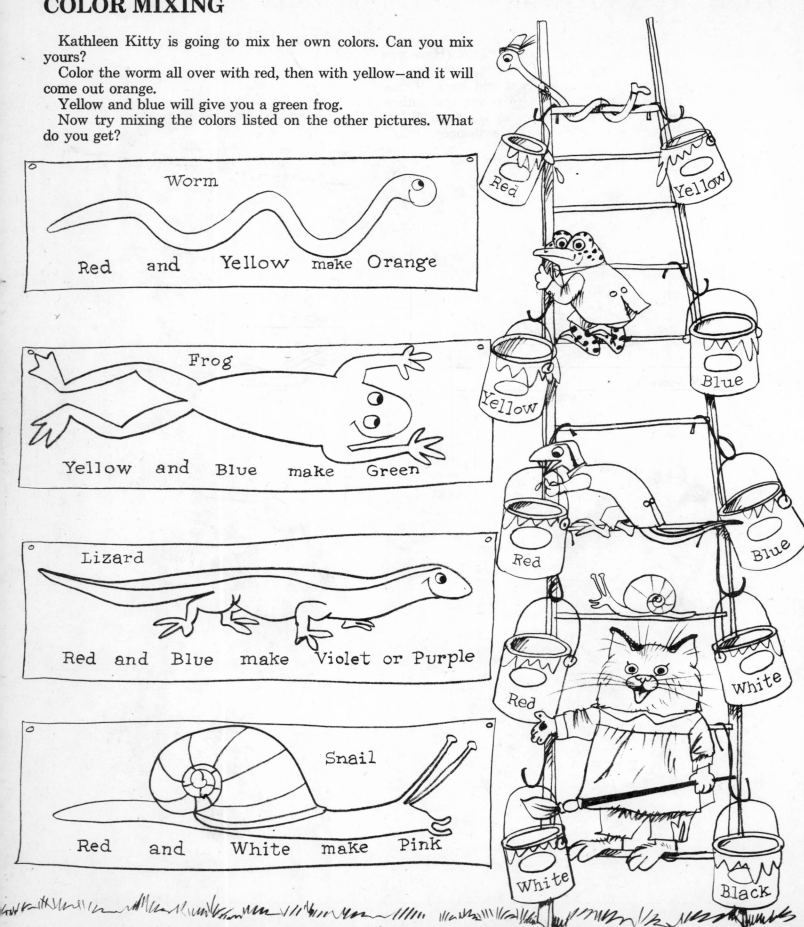

Worm

Red and Yellow make Orange

Frog

Yellow and Blue make Green

Lizard

Red and Blue make Violet or Purple

Snail

Red and White make Pink

THANK-YOU NOTES AND GREETING CARDS

You can use these cards to say "thank you" for presents . . . "get well quick" to a sick friend . . . or to write a short, friendly note. (Have you thanked everyone for your Christmas presents?)

Color the pictures on the cards, front and back. Write your message on the back, on the ruled lines. Cut out the cards, following the outline on this side of the page.

Find the matching envelopes on this page or page 27. Card A goes with Envelope A, etc. Directions for making the envelopes are on page 27.

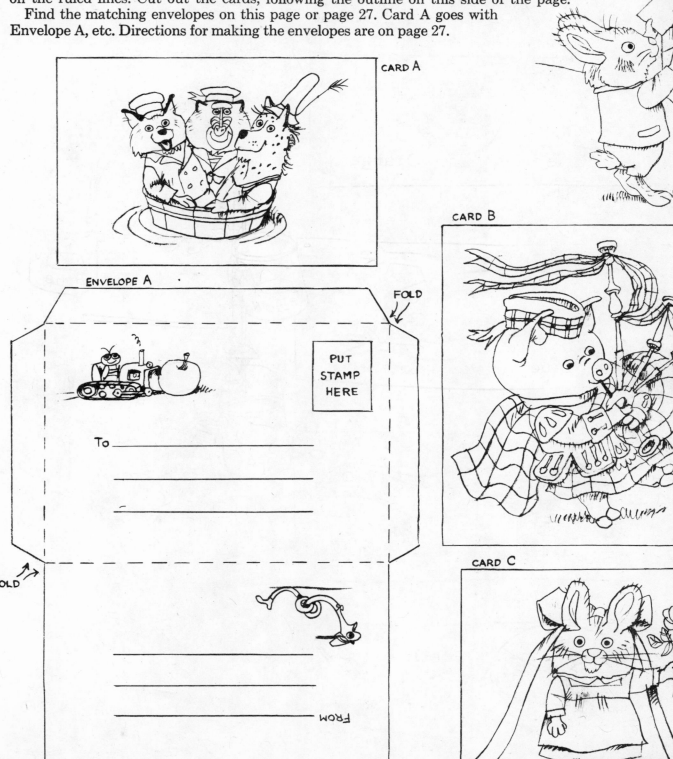

CARD A

CARD B

ENVELOPE A

FOLD

PUT STAMP HERE

To _____

FOLD

FROM

CARD C

Remember—do your cutting
on the other side of the page.

PASTE LAST

PASTE

PASTE

How to make the envelopes for your greeting cards:

Color the pictures on this side of the page. Color the stripes on the other side of the page. Cut each envelope out along the solid black lines. Fold along the dotted lines.

Paste or tape the side tabs to the back of the envelope. Put your card into the envelope, then paste or tape the top tab to the back of the envelope. Address the envelope and put a stamp on it. Then you can mail it.

127,963
127,964

From
Betty Bear
Busytown

To Grandma Bear
West Street
Workville

FOLD

PUT STAMP HERE

PUT STAMP HERE

To _____

To _____

FOLD

FROM

FROM

ENVELOPE C

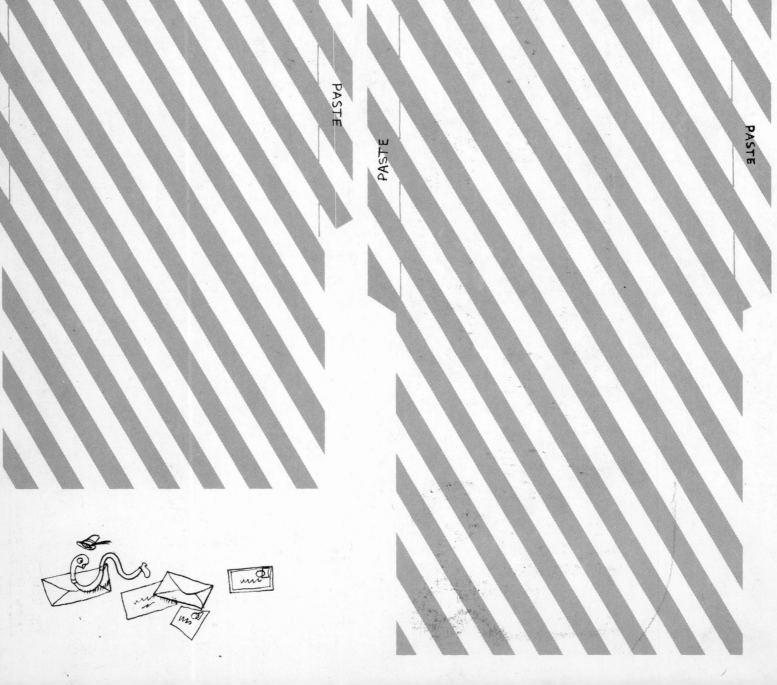

Do your cutting on the other side of the page.

PASTE LAST

PASTE LAST

PASTE

PASTE

PASTE

PASTE

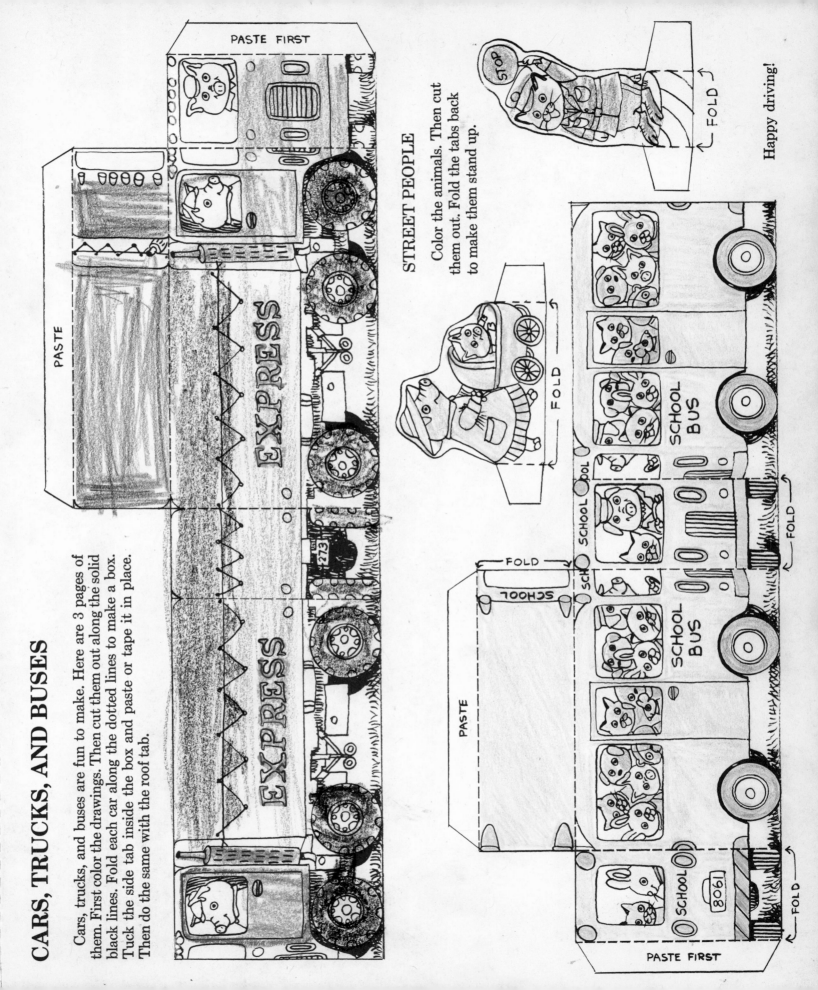

CARS, TRUCKS, AND BUSES

Cars, trucks, and buses are fun to make. Here are 3 pages of them. First color the drawings. Then cut them out along the solid black lines. Fold each car along the dotted lines to make a box. Tuck the side tab inside the box and paste or tape it in place. Then do the same with the roof tab.

PASTE FIRST

PASTE

EXPRESS

EXPRESS

273

STREET PEOPLE

Color the animals. Then cut them out. Fold the tabs back to make them stand up.

STOP

FOLD

Happy driving!

FOLD

SCHOOL BUS

SCHOOL

SCHOOL

FOLD

FOLD

SCHOOL BUS

SCHOOL BUS

PASTE

FOLD

SCHOOL

PASTE FIRST

FOLD

8061

29

Remember—do your cutting on the other side of the page.

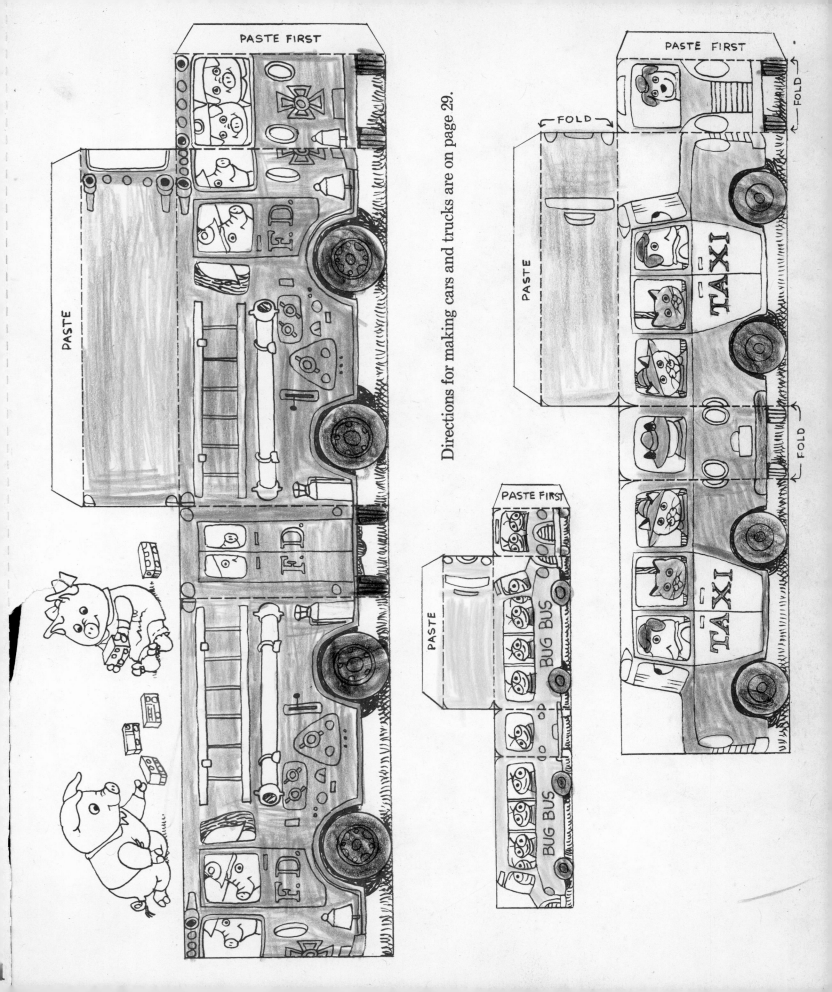

PASTE FIRST

PASTE FIRST

FOLD

FOLD

PASTE

FOLD

Directions for making cars and trucks are on page 29.

PASTE

F.D.

F.D.

F.D.

F.D.

TAXI

TAXI

PASTE FIRST

PASTE

BUG BUS

BUG BUS

BUG BUS

Remember—do your cutting on the other side of the page.

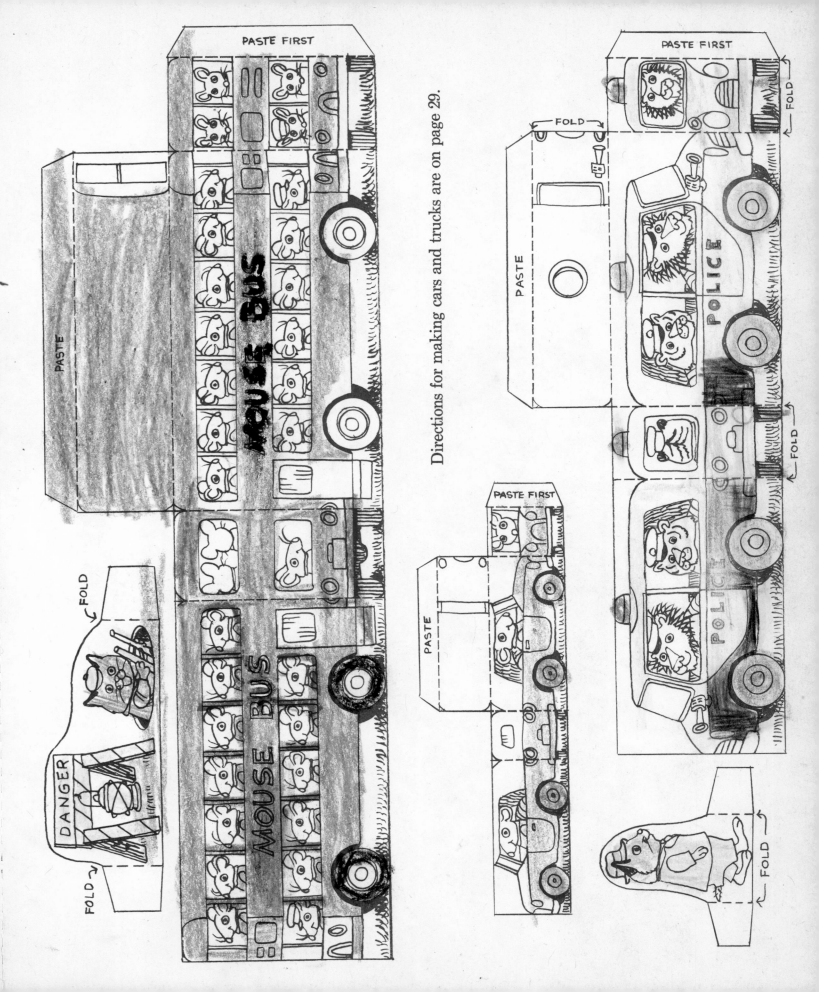

Directions for making cars and trucks are on page 29.

PASTE FIRST

MOUSE BUS

MOUSE BUS

DANGER

FOLD

FOLD

PASTE

POLICE

POLICE

PASTE FIRST

PASTE FIRST

FOLD

FOLD

FOLD

PASTE

3

Remember—do your cutting on the other side of the page. ❖

28 DAYS (29 IN LEAP YEAR — 1976, 1980, 1984, etc.)	FEBRUARY				VALENTINE'S DAY — FEB. 14 GEO. WASHINGTON'S BIRTHDAY — FEB. 22	
SUNDAY	MONDAY	TUESDAY	WEDNESDAY	THURSDAY	FRIDAY	SATURDAY
						1
2	3	4	5	6	7	8
9	10	11	12			
16	17	18	19	20	21	22
23	24	25	26	27	28	

What are Huckle, Lowly, and Rudolf sitting in?
Connect the dots and find out.

VALENTINES

Harry Bear wants to say "I like you" to a friend on Valentine's Day, so he is making a valentine. You can make one, too.

Color the heart, front and back. Be sure to use some red. Go over the dotted lines of writing with a color. Fill in "To" and "From" on the back.

Cut out the heart, following the outline on this side of the page.

Give your valentine on February 14.

Be My Valentine

Cut out heart on the
other side of the page.

MORE VALENTINES

Color the cards, front and back.
Fill in "To" and "From" on the back.
Cut out the cards, following the
outline on this side of the page.

Here are some extra
hearts to color red.

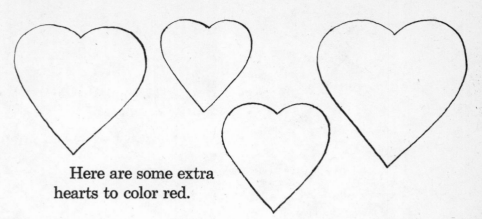

Cut out your valentines on the other side of the page.

To _____

Roses are red, violets are blue
Sugar is sweet, and so are you!.

FROM _____

To _____

FROM _____

Won't you be my valentine?

BE MY
VALENTINE

To _____

FROM _____

Let's take a walk!

Help! Help!
Save Mother Cat!
Huckle, come down
from the attic
at once!

31 DAYS

MARCH

ST. PATRICK'S DAY — MAR. 17

SUNDAY	MONDAY	TUESDAY	WEDNESDAY	THURSDAY	FRIDAY	SATURDAY
						1
2	3	4	5	6	7	8
9	10	11	12	13	14	15
16	17	18	19	20	21	22
23 / 30	24 / 31	25	26	27	28	29

What a big
birthday cake!

BIRTHDAY CARDS

Are you going to a birthday party? You can make your own card to go with your present.

Color the card, front and back.

Sign your name on the back.

Cut out the card, following the outline on this side of the page.

Slip your card under the ribbon on the birthday present.

Have a good time at the party!

Cut out the cards on the other side of the page.

Happy Birthday

FROM _____

HAPPY BIRTHDAY

FROM _____

BUGDOZER

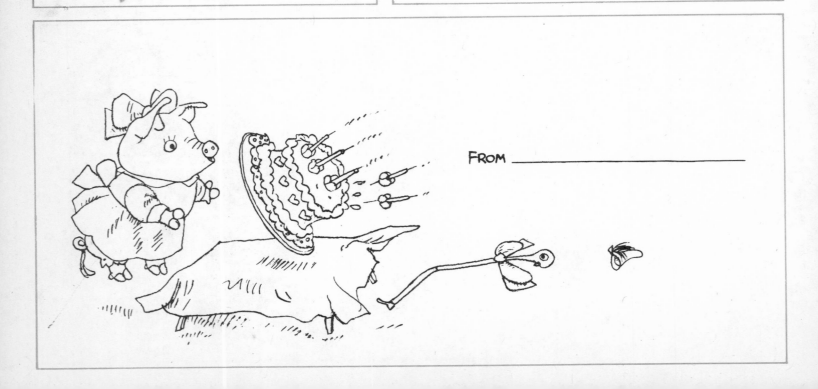

FROM _____

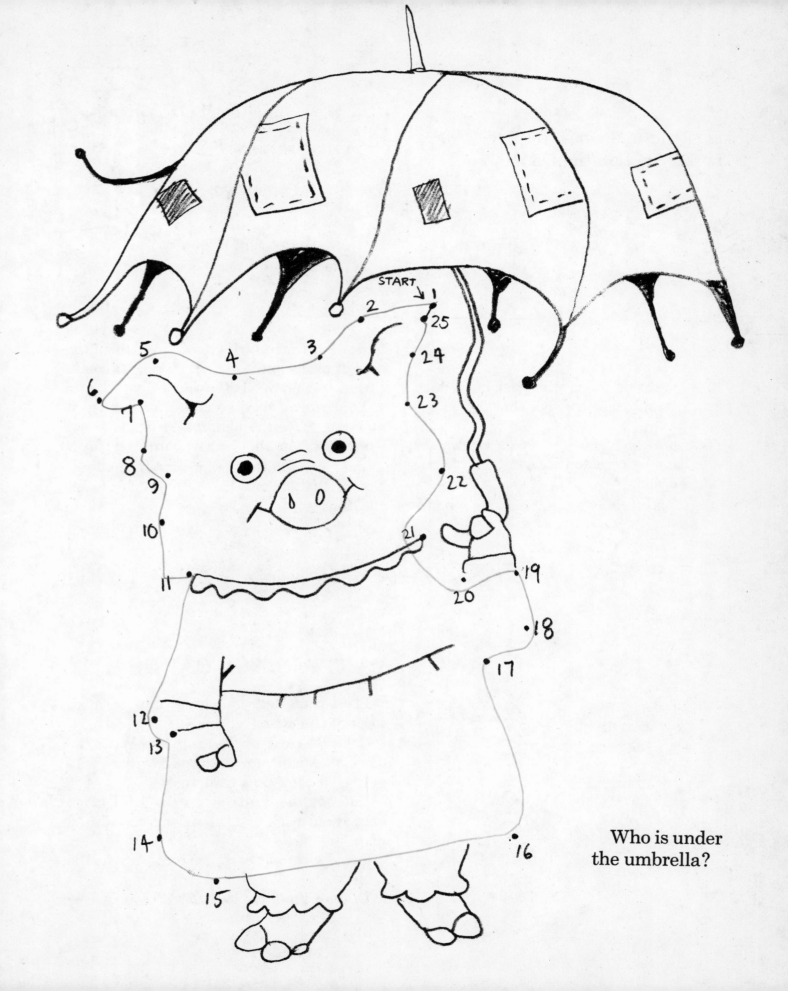

START

Who is under the umbrella?

Do you know how to play
Pin the Tail on the Donkey?

A PARTY GAME

Color the tails on the next page. Color the donkey on page 53.

Cut out the tails along the black lines. Stick pins or thumbtacks through the "X" on the tails.

Tear out the whole donkey page. Tape or paste it on heavy paper or cardboard. Hang it on the wall.

Each player takes a tail. Each one is blind-folded in turn and tries to pin the tail on the correct place on the donkey. Whoever comes closest to the "X" is the winner.

You can make the game even harder if you like. Have the blindfolded player stand 6 or 8 feet from the donkey. Turn the player around 3 times, then point him in the direction of the donkey. He will be lucky to hit the donkey at all!

PARTY PLACE CARDS

Place cards tell your party guests where to sit at the table.

Color the cards on the next page. Write the name of each of your guests on a card. (Write your own name on a card, too!)

Cut out the cards along the solid black lines. Fold back the tabs along the dotted lines.

Stand a card at each person's place at the table.

Doesn't the table look nice?

Donkey Tails

Place Cards

FOLD

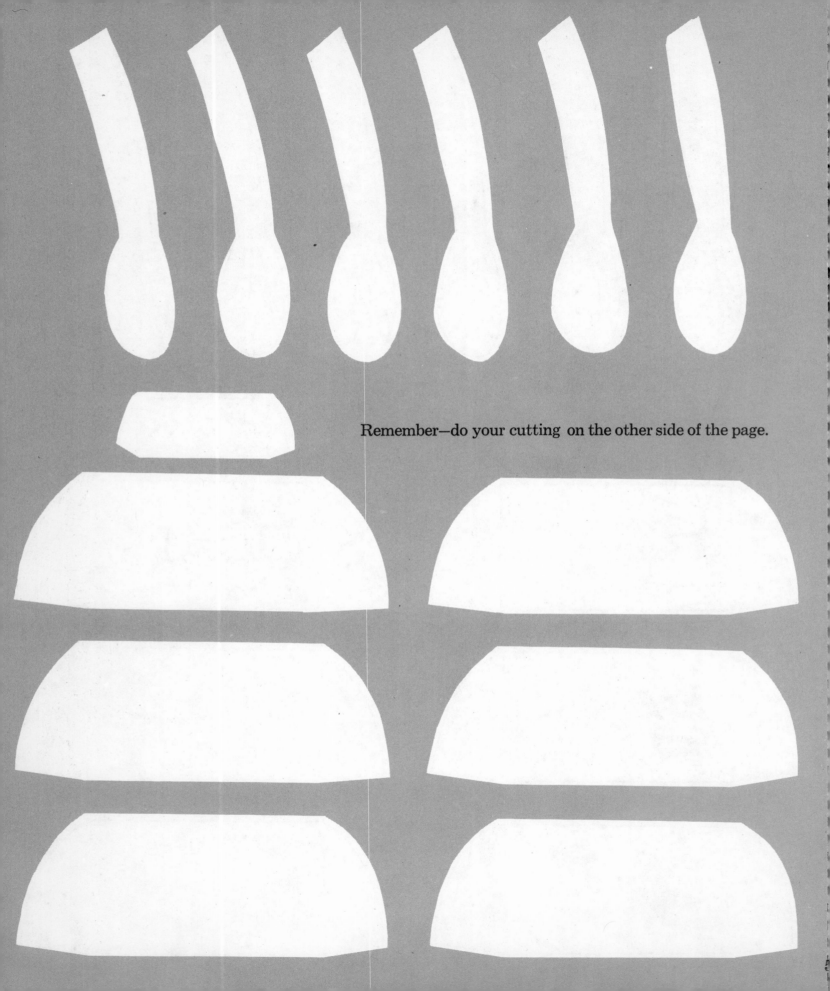

Remember—do your cutting on the other side of the page.

PASTE WHOLE PAGE

a Jet pilot

a poet writing poems

an artist painting a picture

a story writer

a violinist

a pretty model

a businessman

a photographer

a secretary

an operator

CAFÉ

THE NEWS

THE REMARKABLE BOOK SHOP
E. KRAMER, PROP.

ABC

a book printer · a newspaper editor

a saleslady

a newspaper reporter

a janitor

Busy people in Busy Town

MAKING A PAPER AIRPLANE

Color the airplane on both sides of the next page.
Tear the whole page out. Fold along the dotted lines as shown below.
Now you are ready to fly!

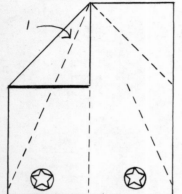

Fold down one top corner.

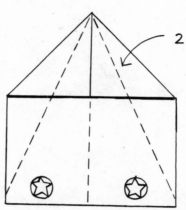

Fold down the other top corner.

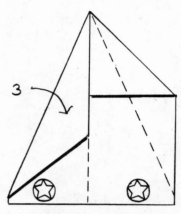

Fold again along the left diagonal dotted line.

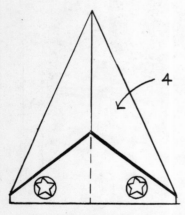

Fold along the right diagonal dotted line.

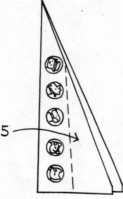

Fold along the center line.

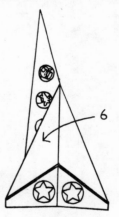

Fold back one wing.

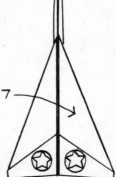

Fold down the other wing.

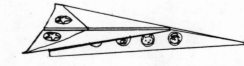

Here is the finished airplane. Hold the nose of the plane together and throw! Sometimes the plane flies best when you bend up the wing tips.

30 DAYS		APRIL			APRIL FOOL'S DAY — APRIL 1	
SUNDAY	MONDAY	TUESDAY	WEDNESDAY	THURSDAY	FRIDAY	SATURDAY
		1	2	3	4	5
6	7	8	9	10	11	12
13	14	15	16	17	18	19
20	21	22	23	24	25	26
27	28	29	30			

START

What has Huckle just seen?
Connect the dots.

6

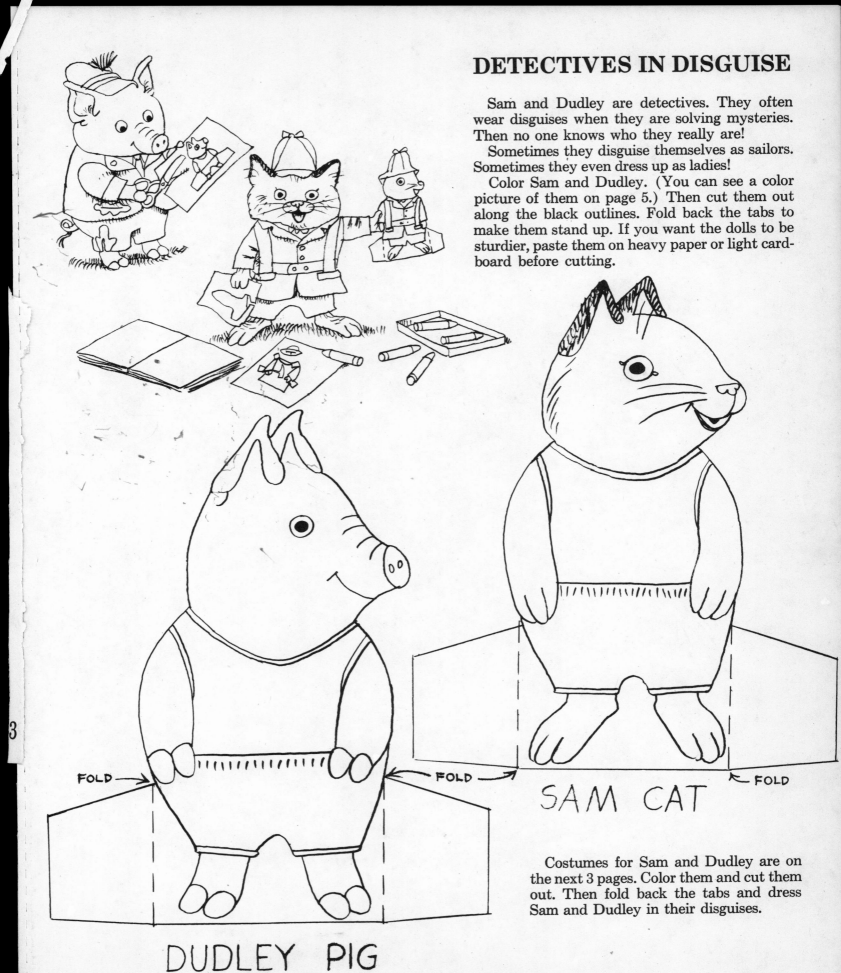

DETECTIVES IN DISGUISE

Sam and Dudley are detectives. They often wear disguises when they are solving mysteries. Then no one knows who they really are!

Sometimes they disguise themselves as sailors. Sometimes they even dress up as ladies!

Color Sam and Dudley. (You can see a color picture of them on page 5.) Then cut them out along the black outlines. Fold back the tabs to make them stand up. If you want the dolls to be sturdier, paste them on heavy paper or light cardboard before cutting.

Costumes for Sam and Dudley are on the next 3 pages. Color them and cut them out. Then fold back the tabs and dress Sam and Dudley in their disguises.

FOLD

FOLD

FOLD

SAM CAT

DUDLEY PIG

Remember—do your cutting on the other side of the page.

SAM CAT

DUDLEY PIG

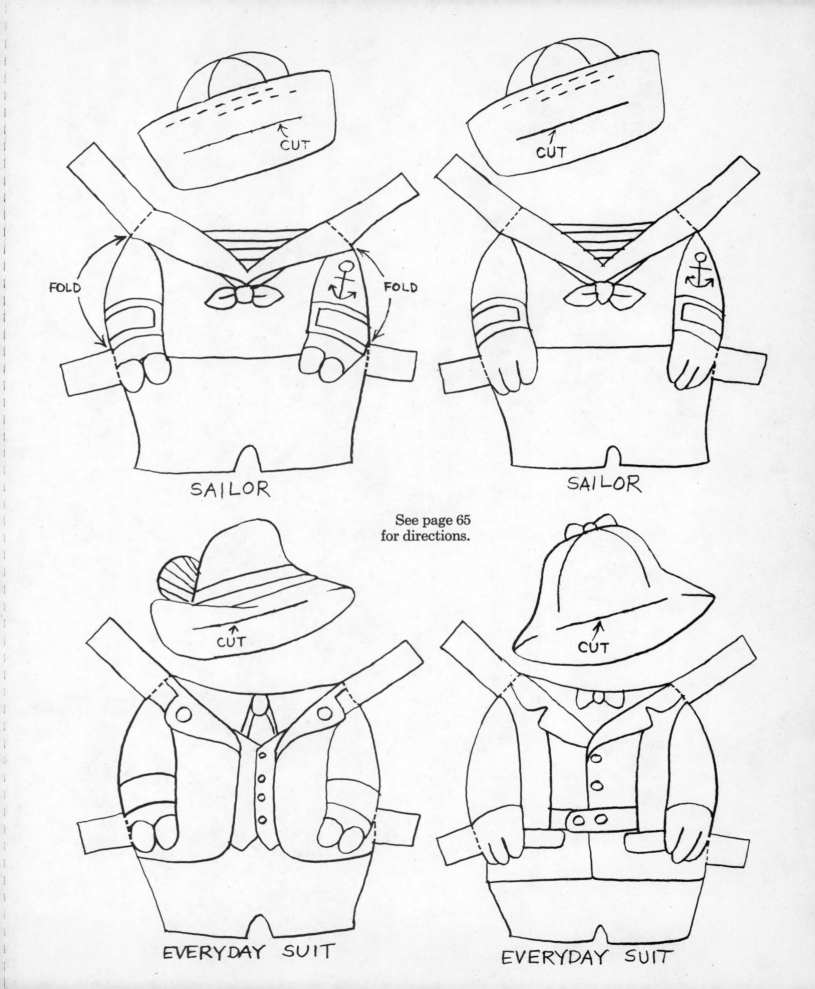

CUT

CUT

FOLD

FOLD

SAILOR

SAILOR

See page 65
for directions.

CUT

CUT

EVERYDAY SUIT

EVERYDAY SUIT

SAM

SAM

DUDLEY

DUDLEY

Do your cutting on
the other side of the page.

SAM

SAM

DUDLEY

DUDLEY

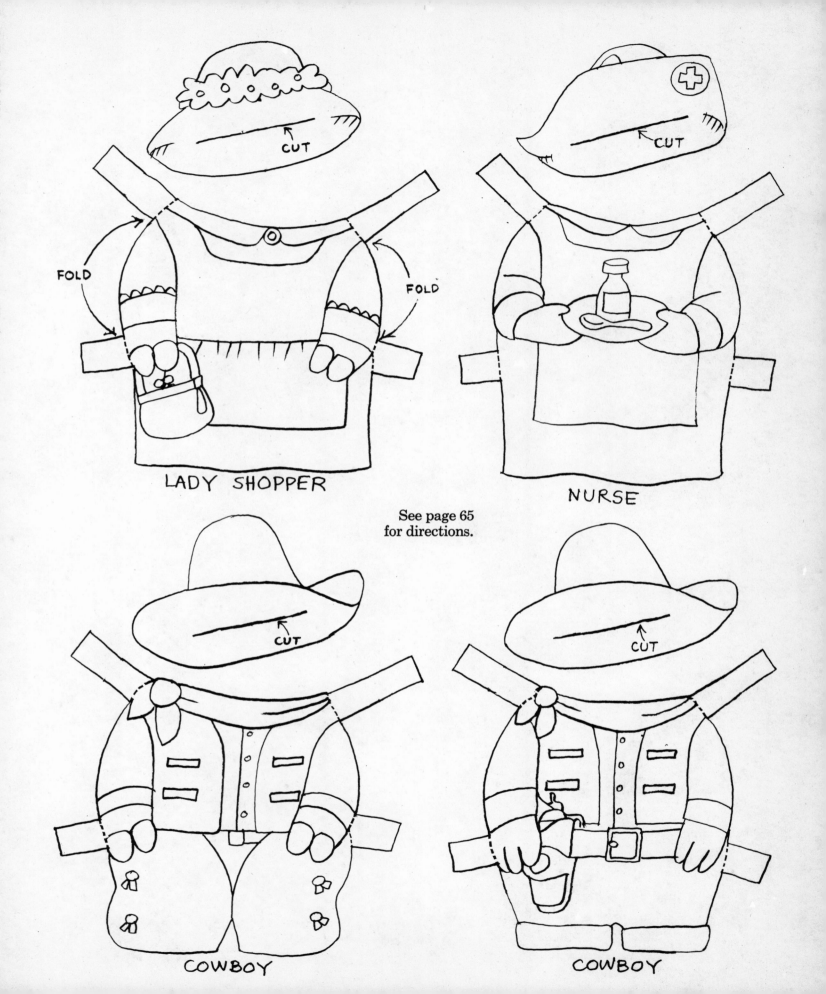

LADY SHOPPER

NURSE

See page 65
for directions.

COWBOY

COWBOY

Do your cutting on
the other side of the page.

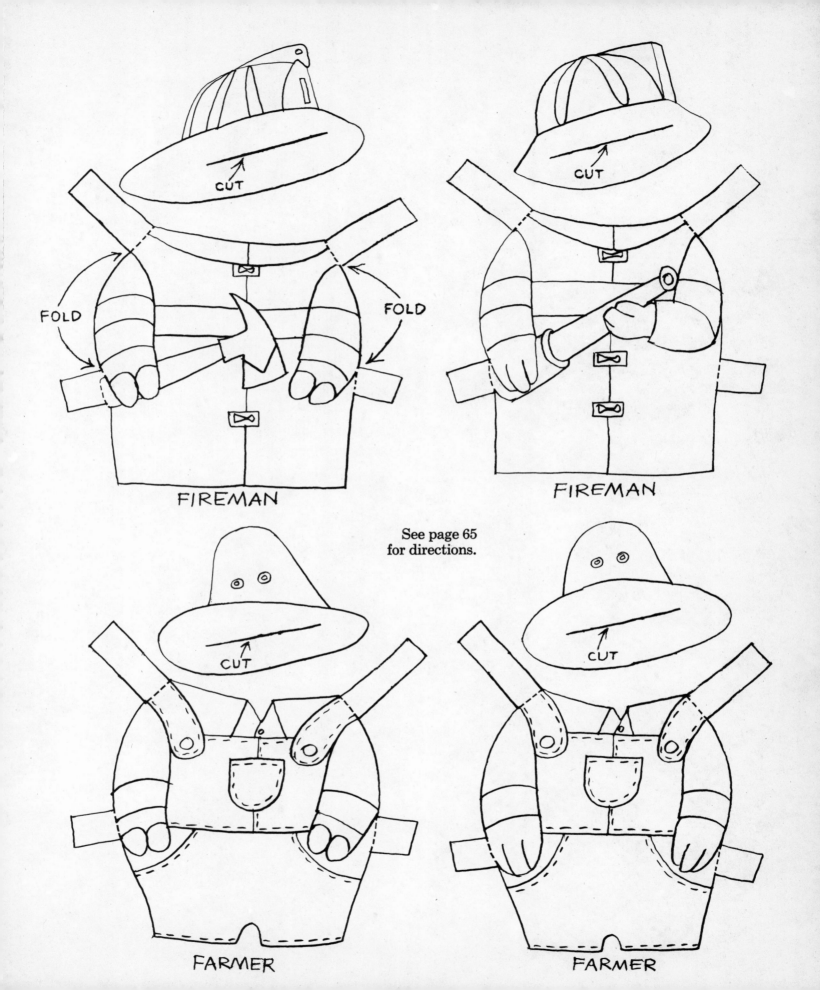

FIREMAN

FIREMAN

See page 65
for directions.

FARMER

FARMER

Do your cutting on
the other side of the page.

SAM

SAM

DUDLEY

DUDLEY

SAM

SAM

DUDLEY

DUDLEY

EASTER CARDS

Color the cards, front and back.
Fill in "To" and "From" on the back.
    Cut the cards out, following the
outlines on this side of the page.
    Hand them out or mail them in envelopes.

Happy
Easter

Happy Easter

HAPPY EASTER

Happy
Easter!

Cut out Easter cards on the other side of the page.

To _____

FROM _____

To _____

FROM _____

To _____

FROM _____

To _____

FROM _____

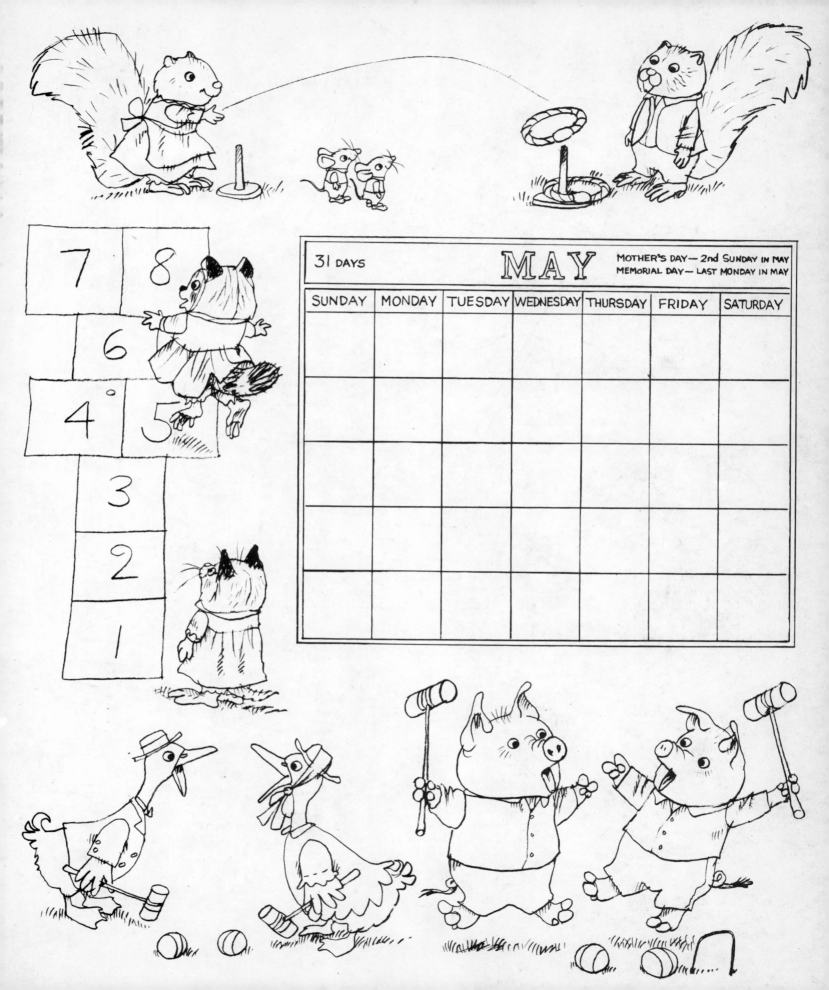

		MAY				
31 DAYS — MOTHER'S DAY — 2nd SUNDAY IN MAY — MEMORIAL DAY — LAST MONDAY IN MAY

SUNDAY	MONDAY	TUESDAY	WEDNESDAY	THURSDAY	FRIDAY	SATURDAY

What a tasty dinner!

FINGER PUPPETS

Color the finger puppets. Cut them out along the outlines.

Bend the tabs around two of your fingers and fasten them with sticky tape.

Wiggle your fingers to make the animals move their heads and talk to each other.

Remember—do your cutting on the other side of the page.

MOTHER'S DAY CARD

Mother's Day is the second Sunday in May. Here is a special card that you can make for your mother.

Color the pictures on the card, front and back. Then cut it out, following the outline on this side of the page. Fold along the dotted line.

Write your name for your mother (Mama, Mommy, etc.) on the front of the card. Sign your name inside.

← FOLD

To

Cut on the other side of the page.

Happy Mother's Day

FROM _____

Farmer Cat likes to drive his tractor.

Who is Lowly Worm holding a chair for?

AIRPLANE MOBILE

Color the planes on this page and the next, on both sides.

Cut the planes out along the outlines.

Gently punch out holes with a pencil.

Tie the planes together with thread or string, just as the picture shows.

Hang them from a stick or wire coat hanger and watch them move in the breeze.

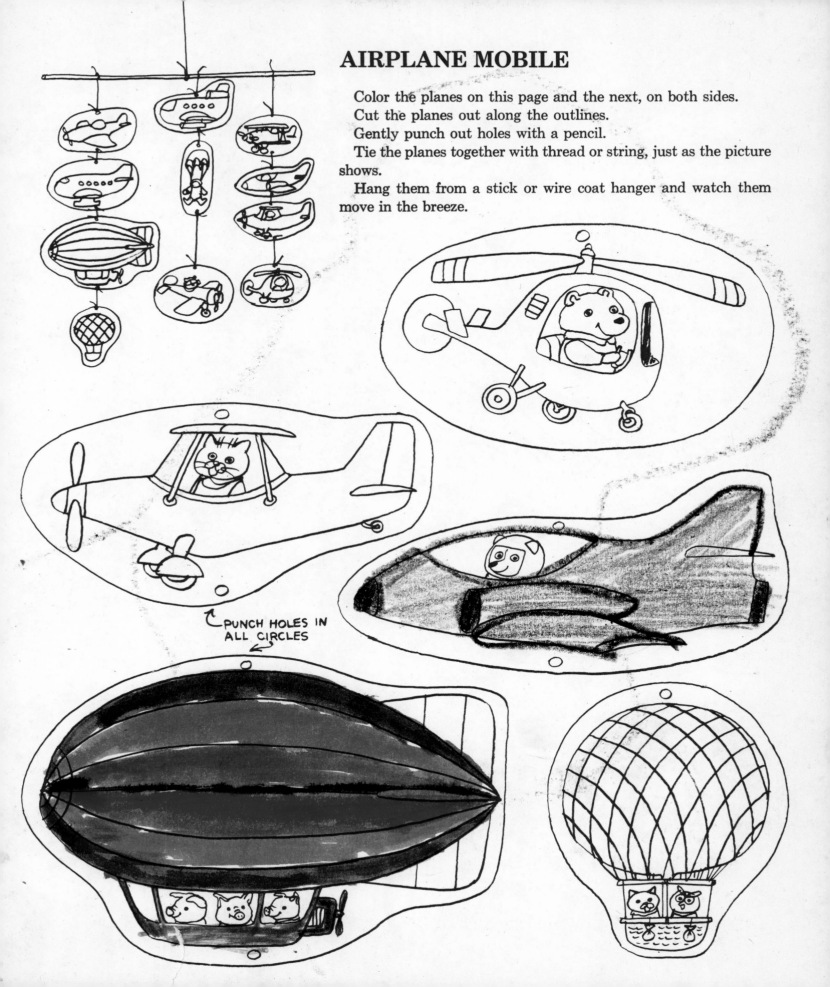

PUNCH HOLES IN ALL CIRCLES

Do your cutting on the other side of the page.

Directions for making an airplane mobile are on page 83.

Do your cutting on the other side of the page.

A nice sunny day at the beach

bath house

1 2 3

beach
umbrella

tent

doll

shovel

pail   sand castle   starfish

The Early Bird meets Bunny Rabbit.

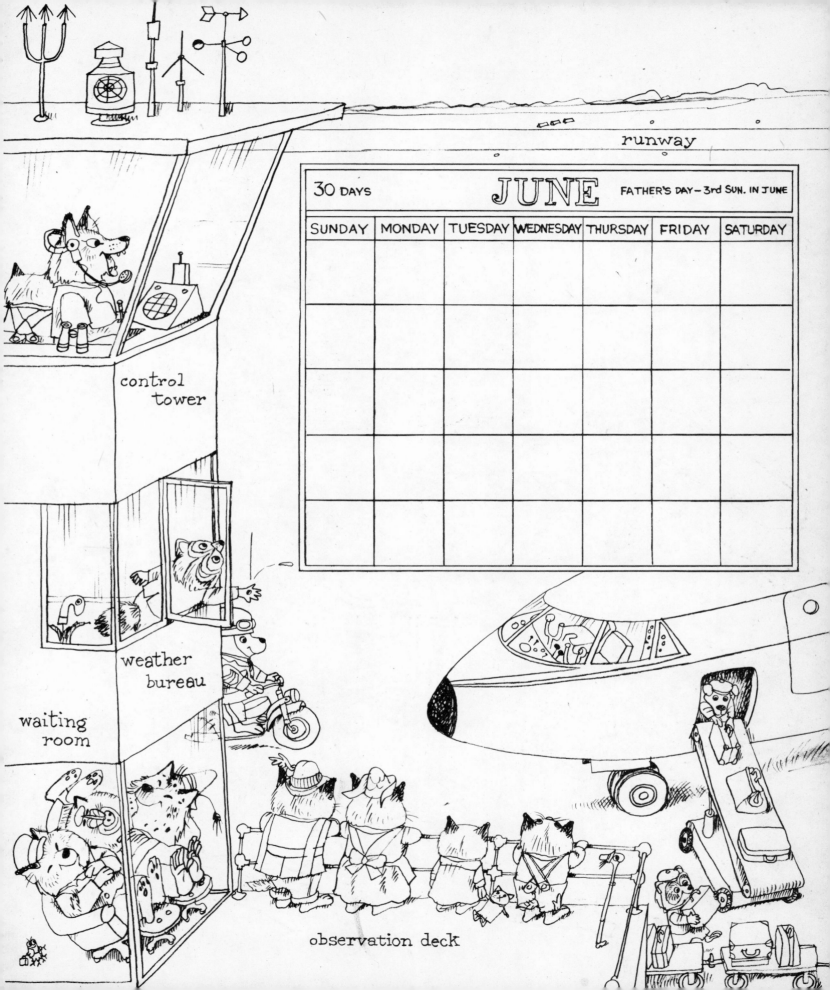

runway

30 DAYS   JUNE   FATHER'S DAY – 3rd SUN. IN JUNE

SUNDAY	MONDAY	TUESDAY	WEDNESDAY	THURSDAY	FRIDAY	SATURDAY

control tower

weather bureau

waiting room

observation deck

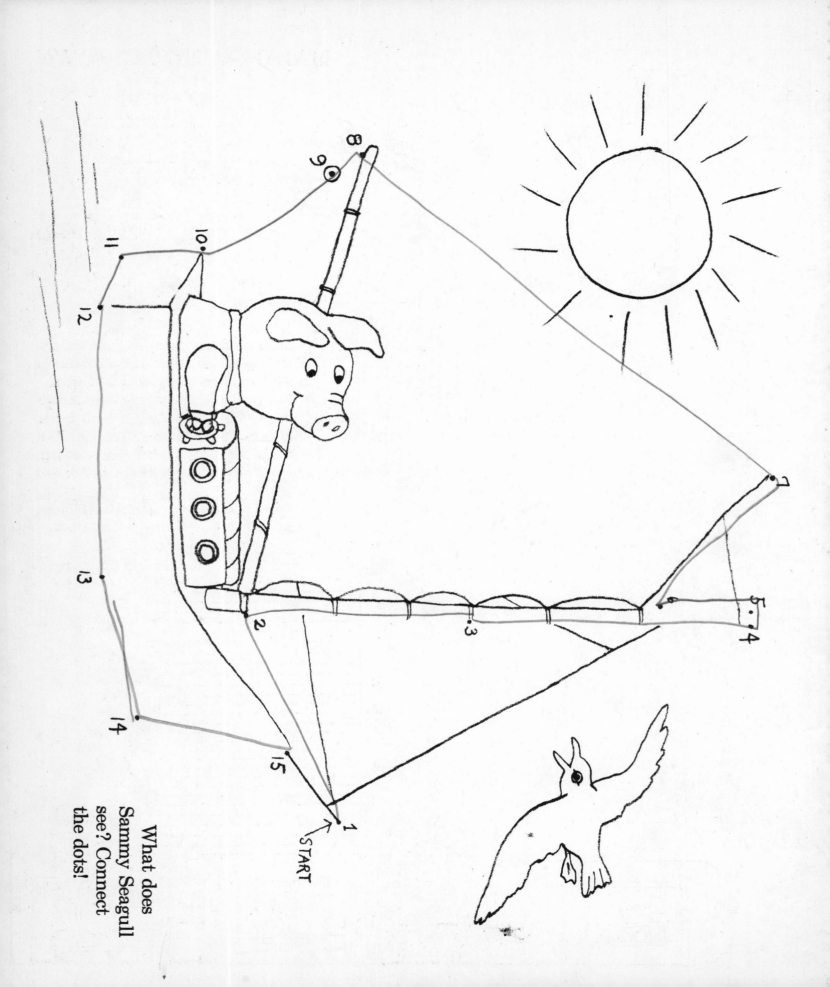

What does Sammy Seagull see? Connect the dots!

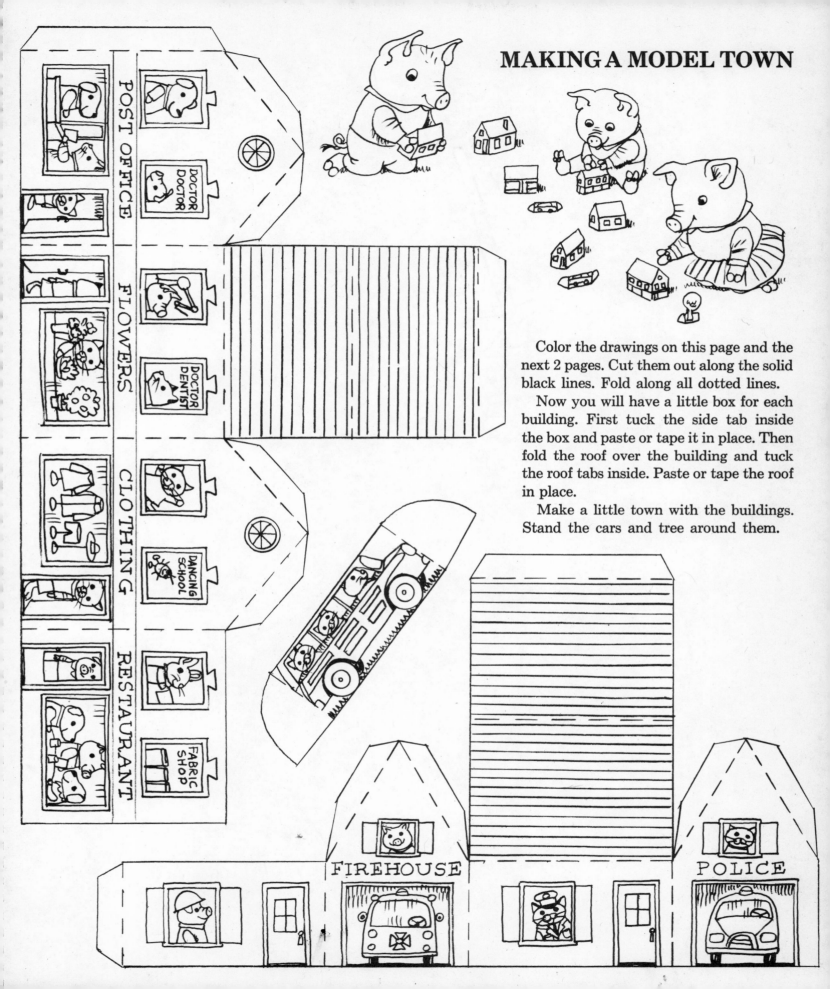

MAKING A MODEL TOWN

POST OFFICE

DOCTOR DOCTOR

FLOWERS

DOCTOR DENTIST

CLOTHING

DANCING SCHOOL

RESTAURANT

FABRIC SHOP

Color the drawings on this page and the next 2 pages. Cut them out along the solid black lines. Fold along all dotted lines.

Now you will have a little box for each building. First tuck the side tab inside the box and paste or tape it in place. Then fold the roof over the building and tuck the roof tabs inside. Paste or tape the roof in place.

Make a little town with the buildings. Stand the cars and tree around them.

FIREHOUSE

POLICE

Remember—do your cutting on the other side of the page.

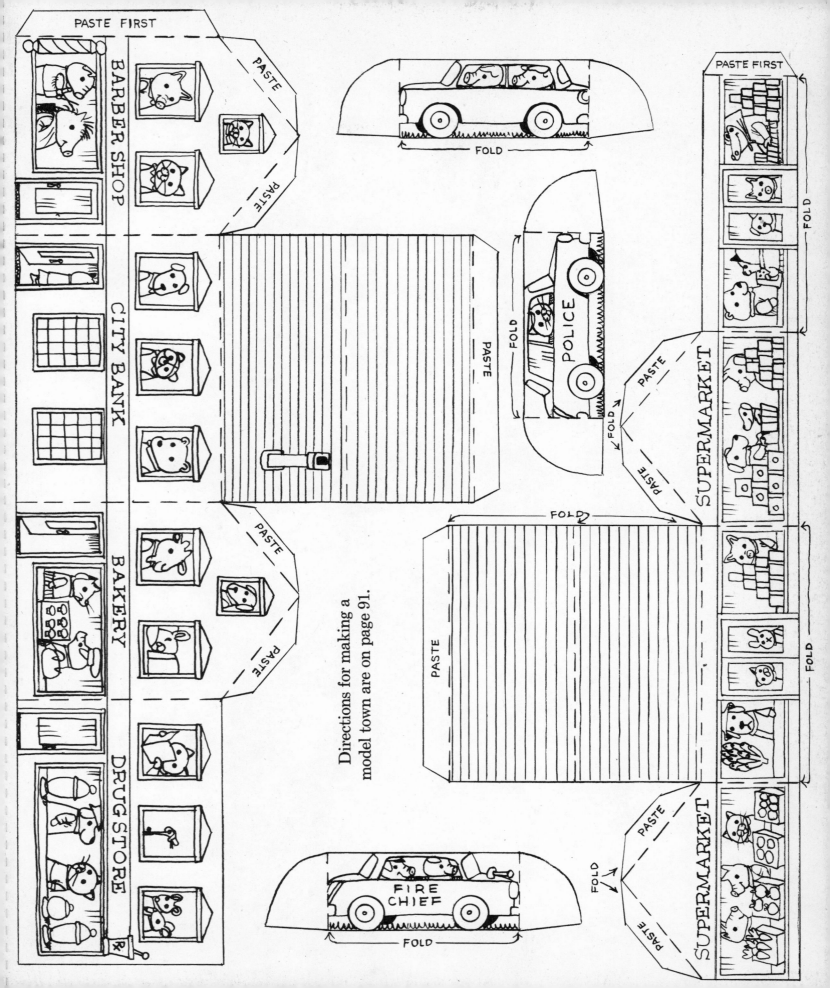

PASTE FIRST

BARBER SHOP

CITY BANK

BAKERY

DRUG STORE

Rx

PASTE

PASTE

PASTE

PASTE

FOLD

POLICE

FOLD

FOLD

PASTE

PASTE

FOLD

PASTE

FOLD

PASTE

PASTE FIRST

FOLD

FOLD

SUPERMARKET

FOLD

FOLD

SUPERMARKET

PASTE

FOLD

PASTE

Directions for making a
model town are on page 91.

FIRE
CHIEF

FOLD

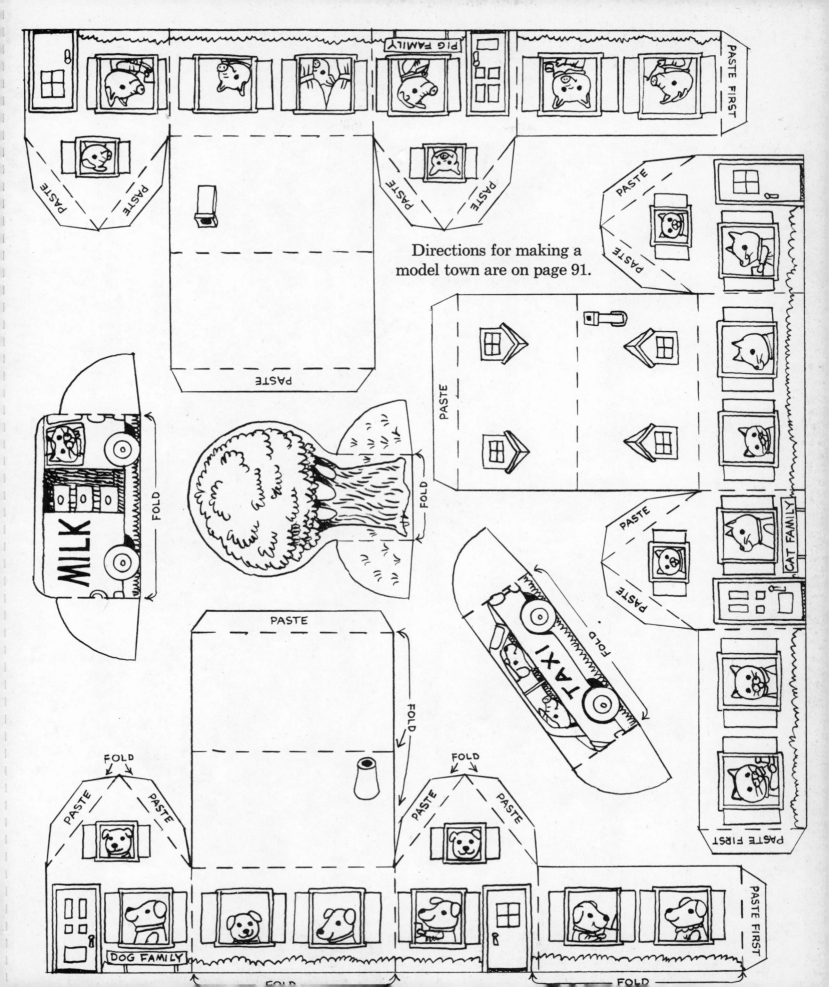

Directions for making a
model town are on page 91.

Remember—do your cutting
on the other side of the page.

FATHER'S DAY CARD

Father's Day is the third Sunday in June. Surprise your father with this funny card.

Color the pictures on the card, front and back.

Then cut it out, following the outline on this side of the page. Fold along the dotted line.

Write your name for your father (Papa, Daddy, etc.) on the front of the card. Sign your name inside.

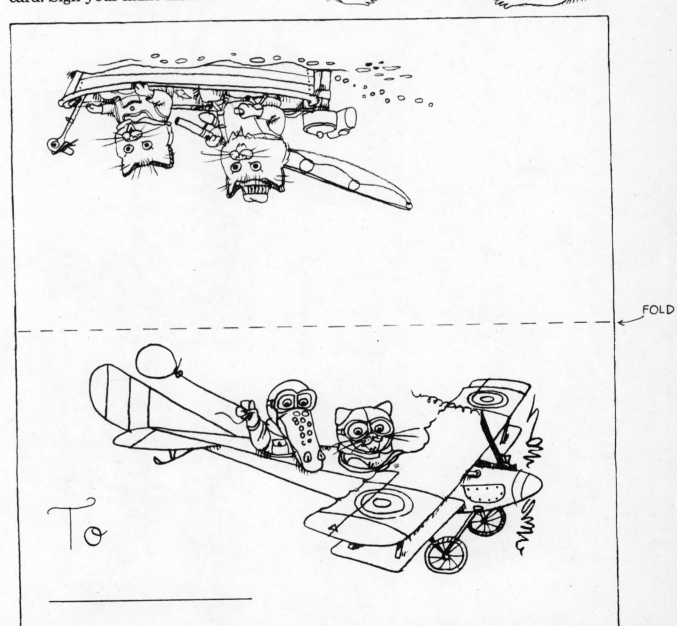

FOLD

To

Cut out card on the other side of the page.

Happy Father's Day

FROM _____

31 DAYS	JULY				INDEPENDENCE DAY — JULY 4	
SUNDAY	MONDAY	TUESDAY	WEDNESDAY	THURSDAY	FRIDAY	SATURDAY

What is happening to that pile of papers?
Connect the dots and find out!

You can see some of these flags in color on page 9.

FLAG DECORATION

Color the flags on this page and the next. Cut them out along the solid black lines. Fold the tabs over a string at least 3 feet long. Tape or paste the tab to the back of each flag. Now you will have a nice decoration to hang in your room.

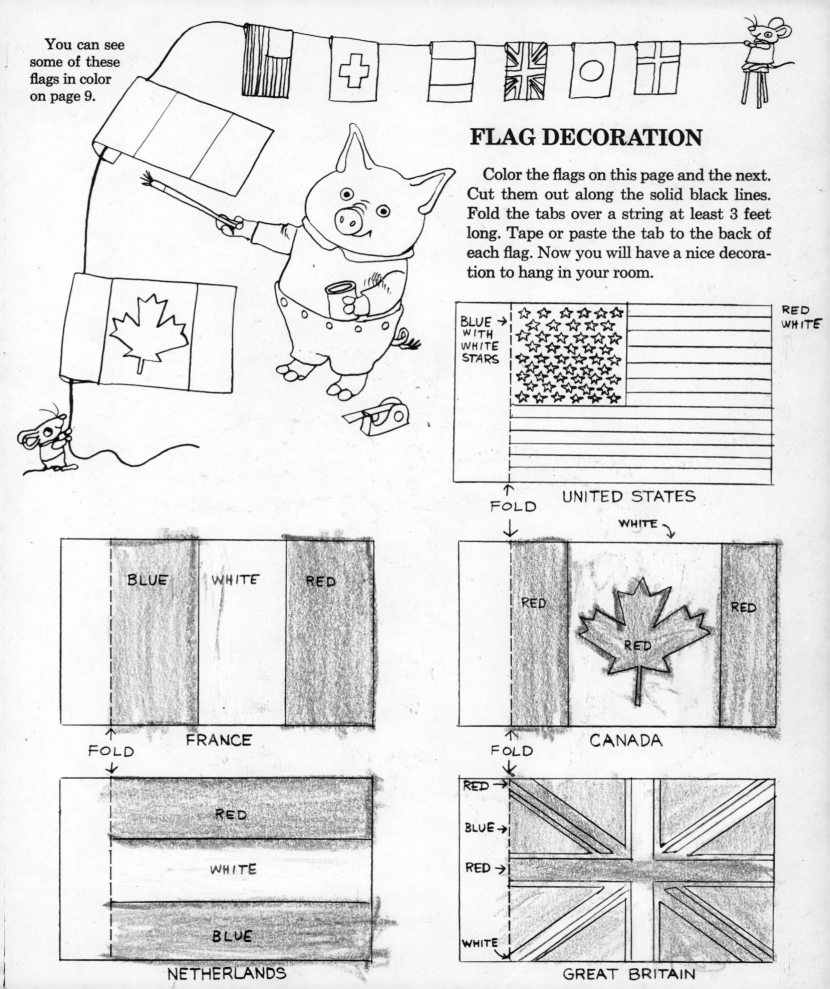

BLUE
WITH
WHITE
STARS

RED
WHITE

↑
FOLD   UNITED STATES

BLUE   WHITE   RED

↑
FOLD   FRANCE

WHITE ↘

RED   RED   RED

↑
FOLD   CANADA

↑
FOLD
↓

RED

WHITE

BLUE

NETHERLANDS

RED →
BLUE →
RED →

WHITE

GREAT BRITAIN

Do your cutting on the other side of the page.

UNITED STATES

PASTE

CANADA

PASTE

FRANCE

PASTE

GREAT BRITAIN

PASTE

NETHERLANDS

PASTE

Directions for making a flag decoration are on page 101.

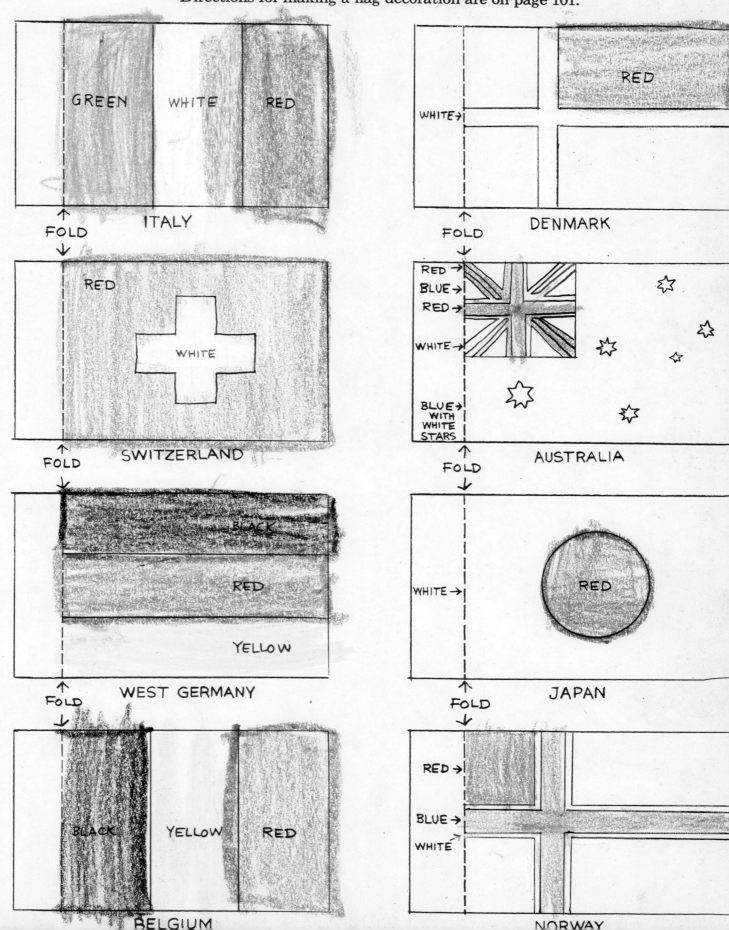

GREEN   WHITE   RED

ITALY

FOLD

RED

WHITE

SWITZERLAND

FOLD

BLACK

RED

YELLOW

WEST GERMANY

FOLD

BLACK   YELLOW   RED

BELGIUM

RED

WHITE →

DENMARK

FOLD

RED →
BLUE →
RED →

WHITE →

BLUE →
WITH
WHITE
STARS

AUSTRALIA

FOLD

WHITE →

RED

JAPAN

FOLD

RED →

BLUE →

WHITE →

NORWAY

8

Do your cutting on the other side of the page.

DENMARK

ITALY

PASTE

AUSTRALIA

SWITZERLAND

PASTE

JAPAN

WEST GERMANY

PASTE

NORWAY

BELGIUM

PASTE

Connect the 3 sets of numbered dots to finish this picture of Tiger Cat.

HOW TO MAKE TWO FLYING CROWS

Color Ma and Pa Crow on the next two pages, on both sides of each page. Use lots of different colors.

Tear out both pages along the perforated lines.

Fold the crows along the dotted lines, as shown below.

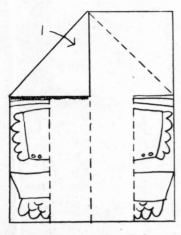 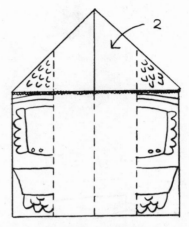

Start with the side of the paper that doesn't show the eyes. Fold down one top corner.

Fold down the other top corner.

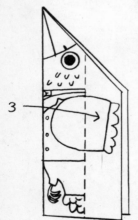 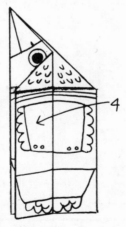 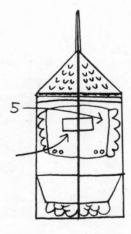

Fold along the center dotted line.

Fold over the top wing.

Fold the other wing. Fasten the two wings together with sticky tape.

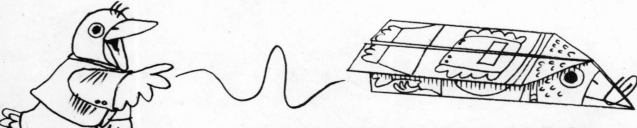

Now the crow is ready to fly. Sometimes it flies better if the beak is held together with a paper clip.

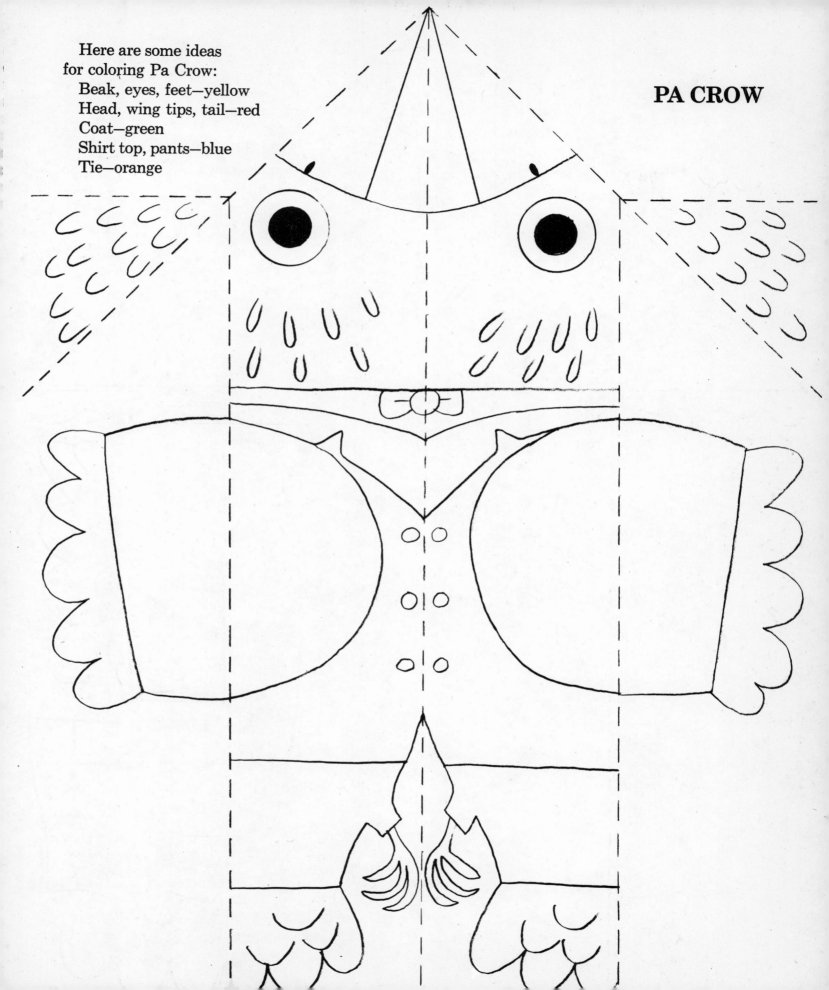

Here are some ideas
for coloring Pa Crow:
Beak, eyes, feet—yellow
Head, wing tips, tail—red
Coat—green
Shirt top, pants—blue
Tie—orange

PA CROW

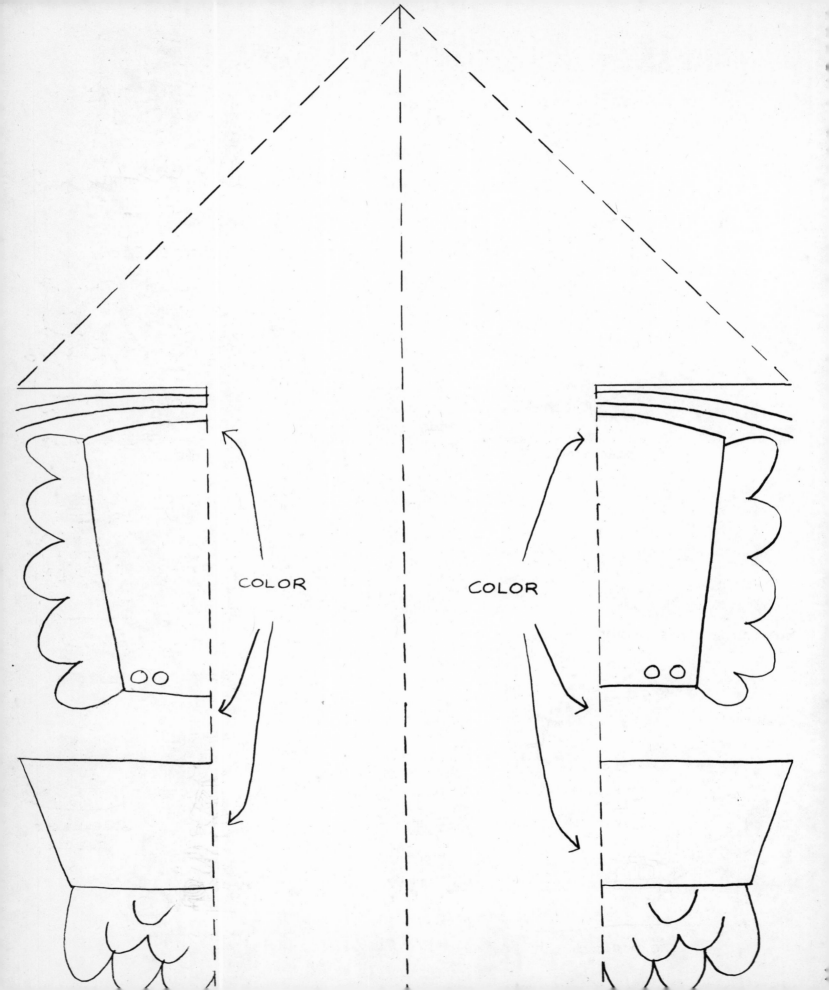

COLOR

COLOR

SOME SPECIAL FRIENDS

Do you know all of these people from Busy Town?
They are saying "hello" to you. Why don't you color
all of them?

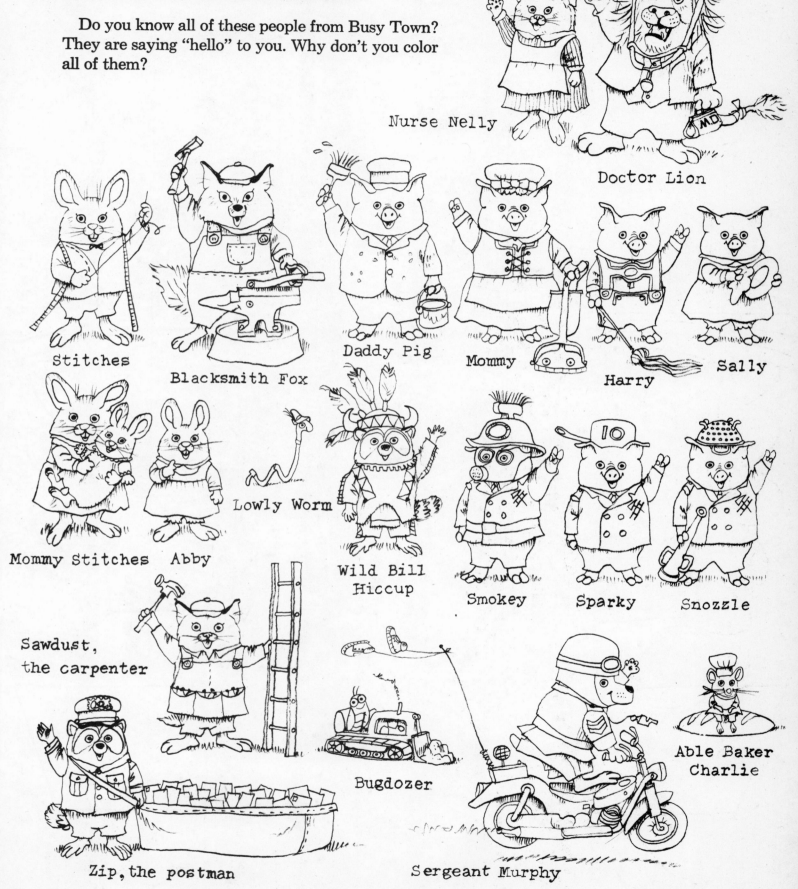

Nurse Nelly

Doctor Lion

Stitches

Blacksmith Fox

Daddy Pig

Mommy

Harry

Sally

Mommy Stitches   Abby

Lowly Worm

Wild Bill
Hiccup

Smokey

Sparky

Snozzle

Sawdust,
the carpenter

Bugdozer

Able Baker
Charlie

Zip, the postman

Sergeant Murphy

The pig family is going on vacation.
Charlie Dog's taxi can barely hold them all!

balloon

DRINK WATER

blimp

EAT BRUNO'S HOT DOGS

BRUNO'S HOT DOGS

LIFE GUARD

life guard

paper plates

31 DAYS AUGUST

SUNDAY	MONDAY	TUESDAY	WEDNESDAY	THURSDAY	FRIDAY	SATURDAY

surfer

waves

Sergeant Murphy rides again!

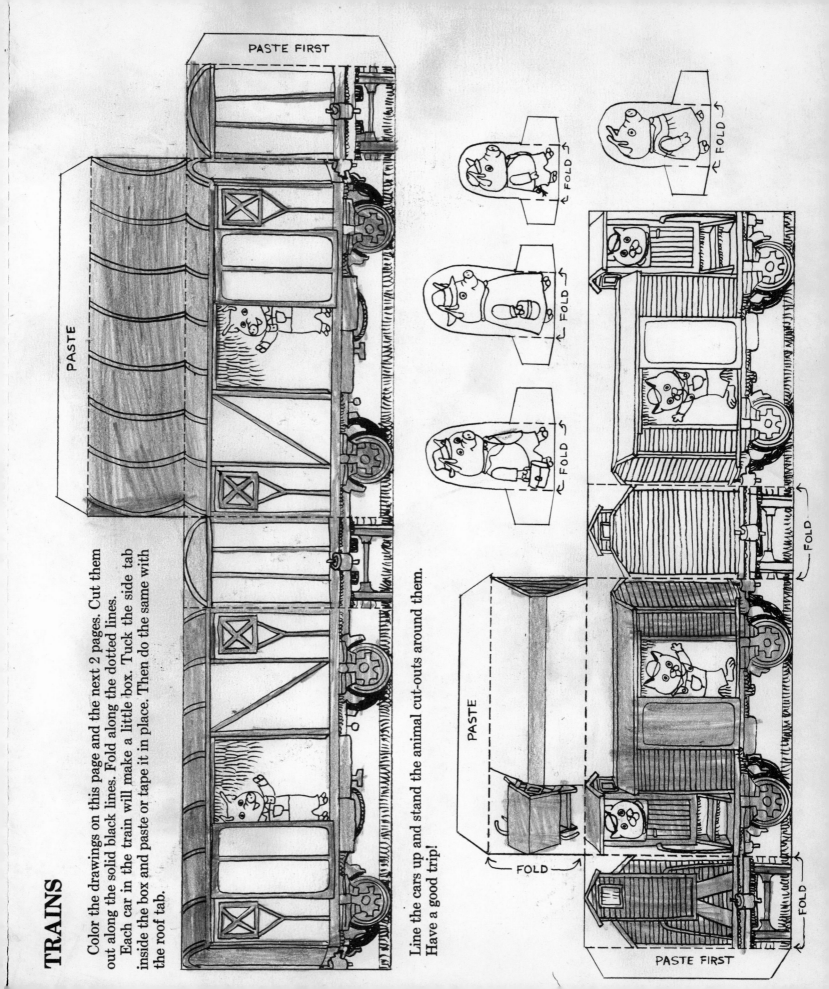

TRAINS

Color the drawings on this page and the next 2 pages. Cut them out along the solid black lines. Fold along the dotted lines.

Each car in the train will make a little box. Tuck the side tab inside the box and paste or tape it in place. Then do the same with the roof tab.

Line the cars up and stand the animal cut-outs around them. Have a good trip!

PASTE FIRST

PASTE

PASTE

PASTE

PASTE FIRST

FOLD

FOLD

FOLD

FOLD

FOLD

FOLD

FOLD

Remember—do your cutting on the other side of the page.

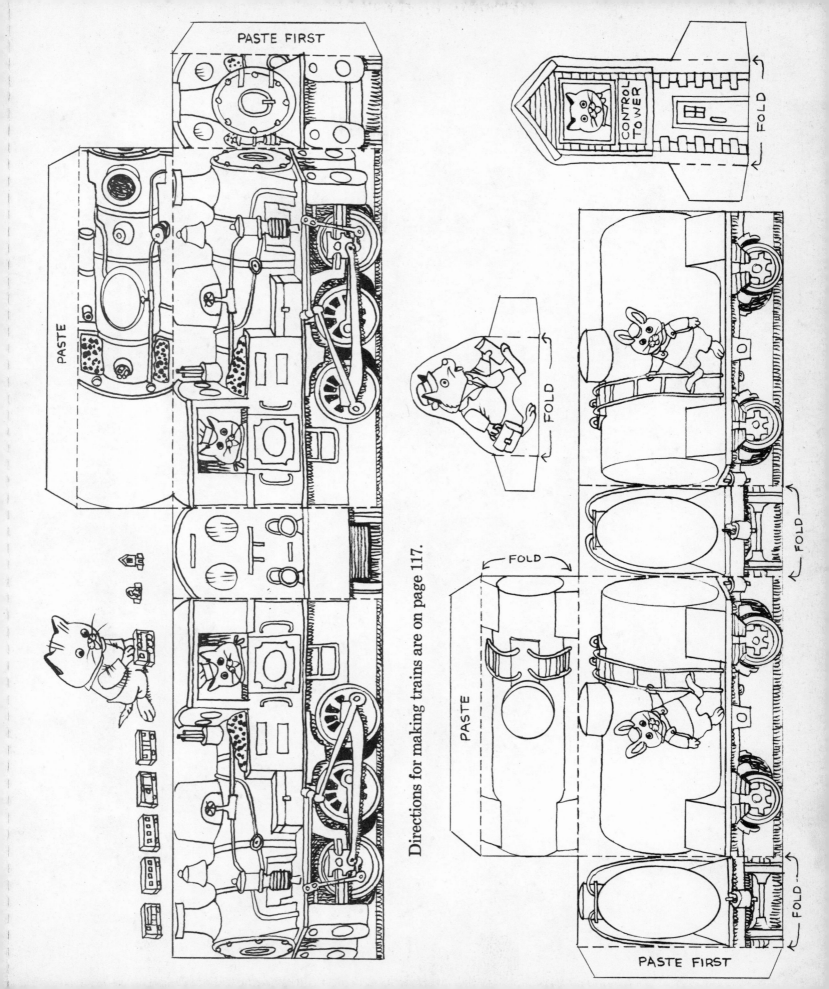

PASTE FIRST

PASTE

CONTROL TOWER

FOLD

FOLD

FOLD

FOLD

FOLD

FOLD

PASTE

Directions for making trains are on page 117.

PASTE FIRST

Remember—do your cutting on the other side of the page.

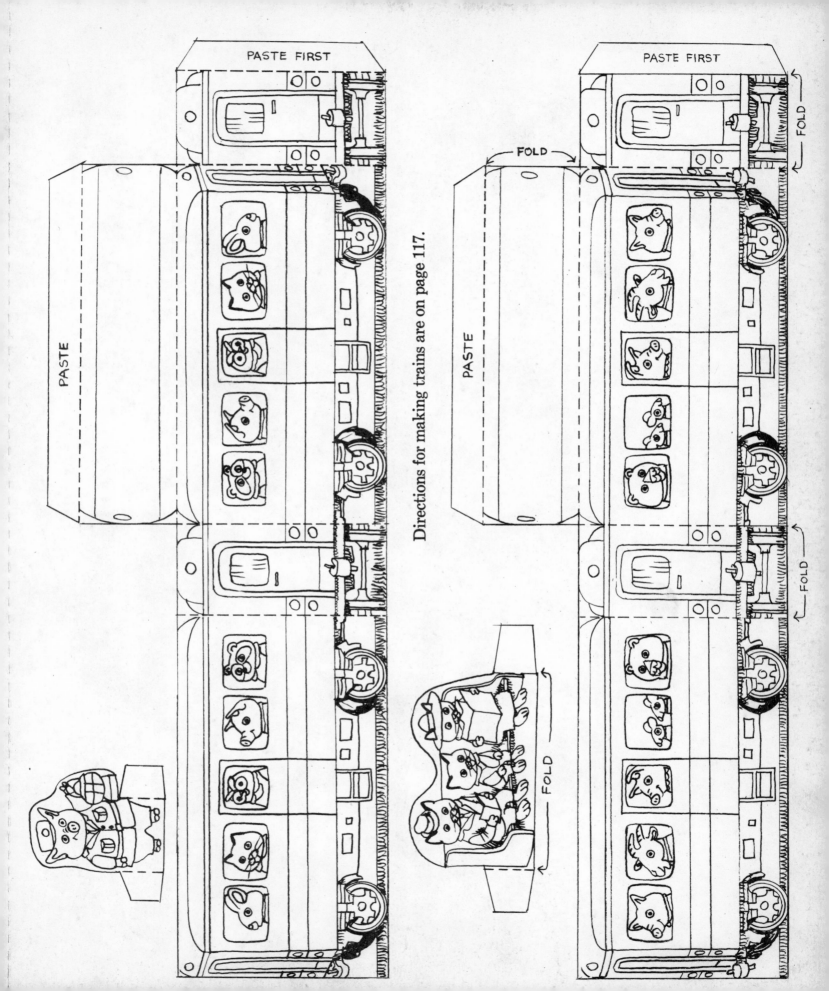

PASTE FIRST

FOLD

PASTE

Directions for making trains are on page 117.

PASTE FIRST

FOLD

FOLD

PASTE

FOLD

Remember—do your cutting on the other side of the page.

Sam Cat and Dudley Pig are detectives.
They dress in many disguises so that
no one will know who they are.
Color the turtle and the garbage can—
but don't tell anyone who is inside them!

Huckle and Lowly Worm
are off to school.
  When do you start school?

SEPTEMBER

30 DAYS

LABOR DAY —
1st MON. IN SEPT.

SUNDAY	MONDAY	TUESDAY	WEDNESDAY	THURSDAY	FRIDAY	SATURDAY

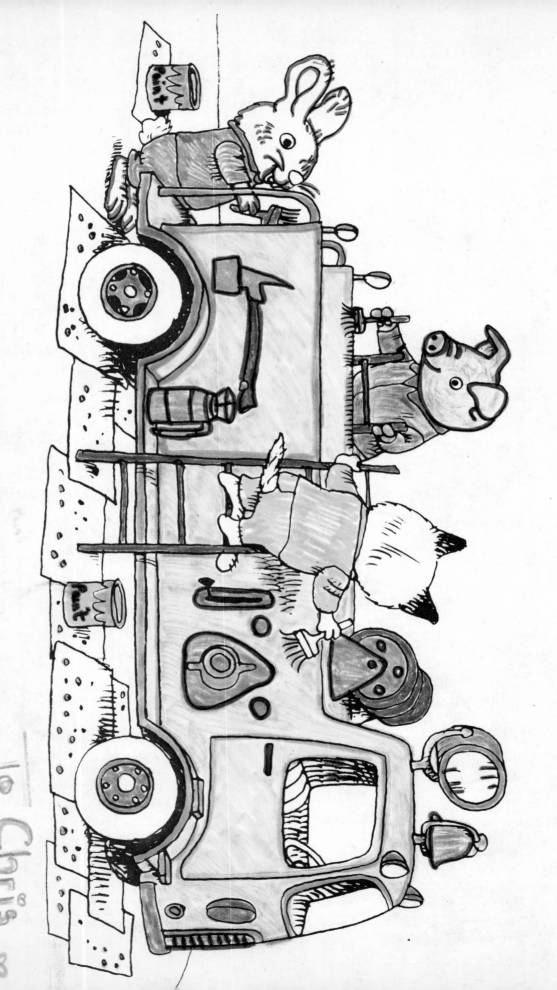

The fire engine needs a new coat of paint. Will you help paint it? You can see it in color on page 2.

To Chris

Love

Mom

BOOKPLATES

Fill in your name and color the pictures. Cut out along the solid black outlines. Paste onto the inside front cover of your own books.

THIS BOOK BELONGS TO
_____
_____

THIS BOOK BELONGS TO

Chris _____

THIS BOOK BELONGS TO
_____

THIS BOOK BELONGS TO
_____

THIS BOOK BELONGS TO

Chris _____

Remember—do your cutting on the other side of the page.

PASTE

PASTE

PASTE

PASTE

PASTE

BOOKMARKS

Color the pictures, front and back. Cut out, following the solid black outlines on this side of the page. Now you can mark your place when you stop reading.

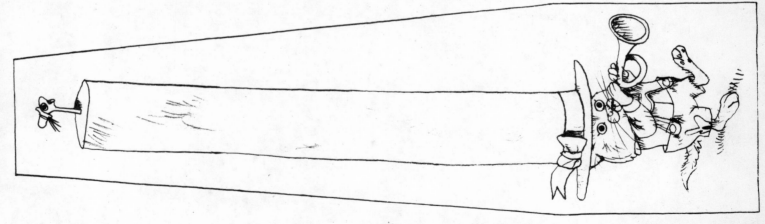

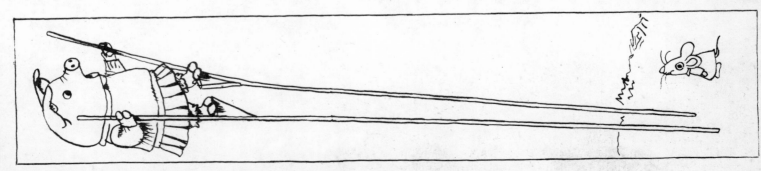

Do your cutting on the other side of the page!

Miss Honey has written the alphabet on the blackboard. Help the children color it in.

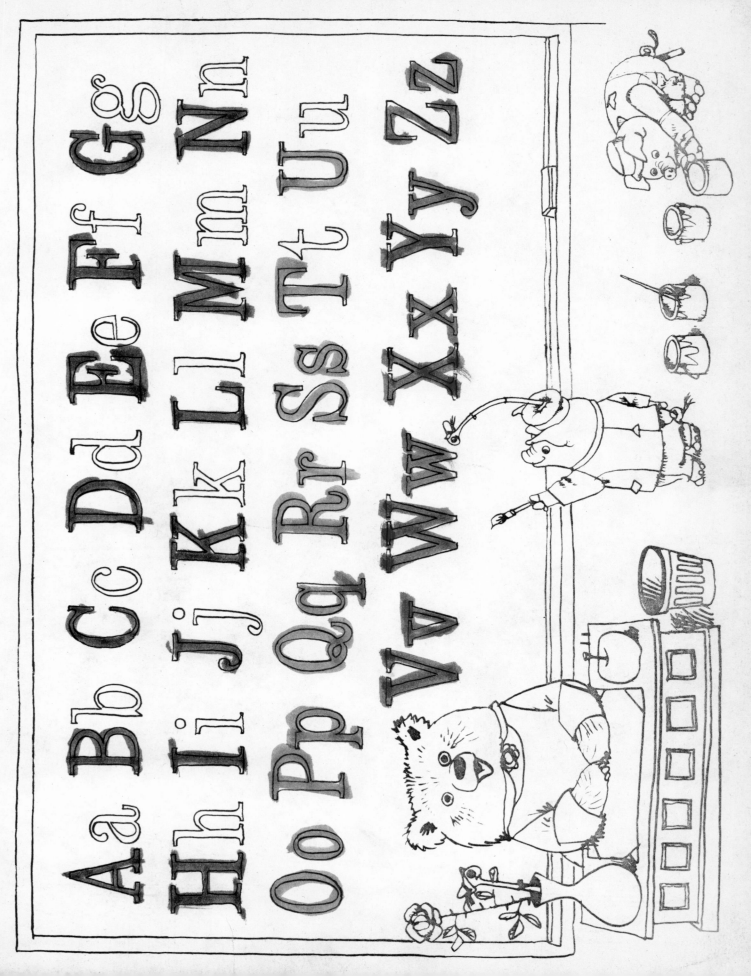

Bruno has a picnic.

Count along with Miss Honey and color the numbers.

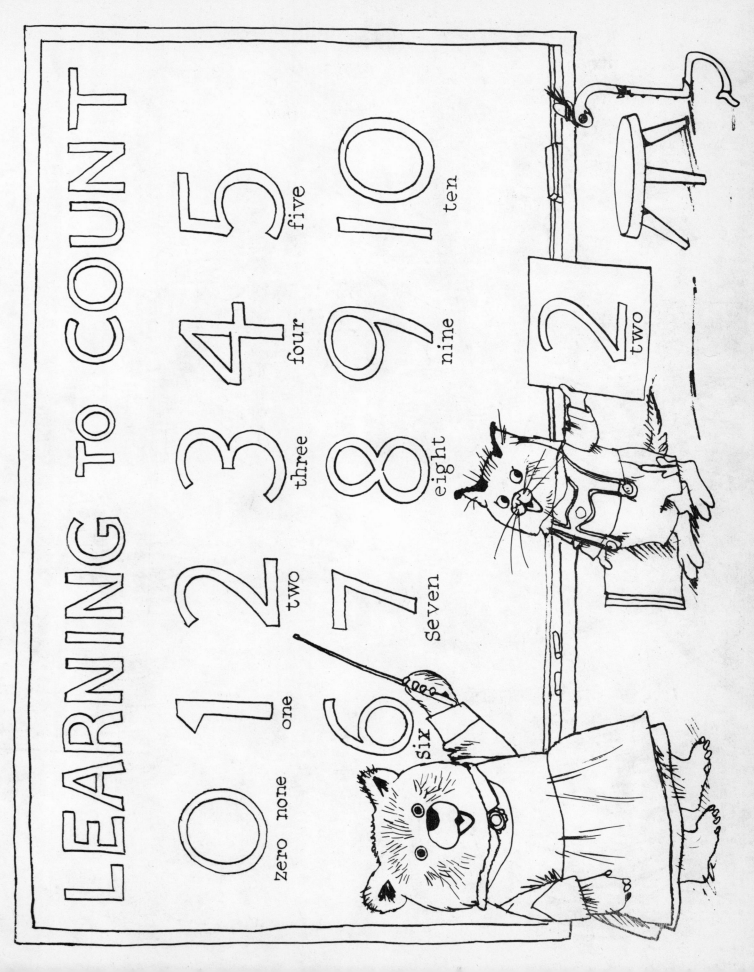

LEARNING TO COUNT

0 1 2
zero none one two

3 4 5
three four five

6 7 8 9 10
six seven eight nine ten

2
two

Mr. Pig likes to read stories to Joseph and Josephine.

This is Busy Town.
My, what a nice town!

START →

What is Loony Gorilla
driving down the street?

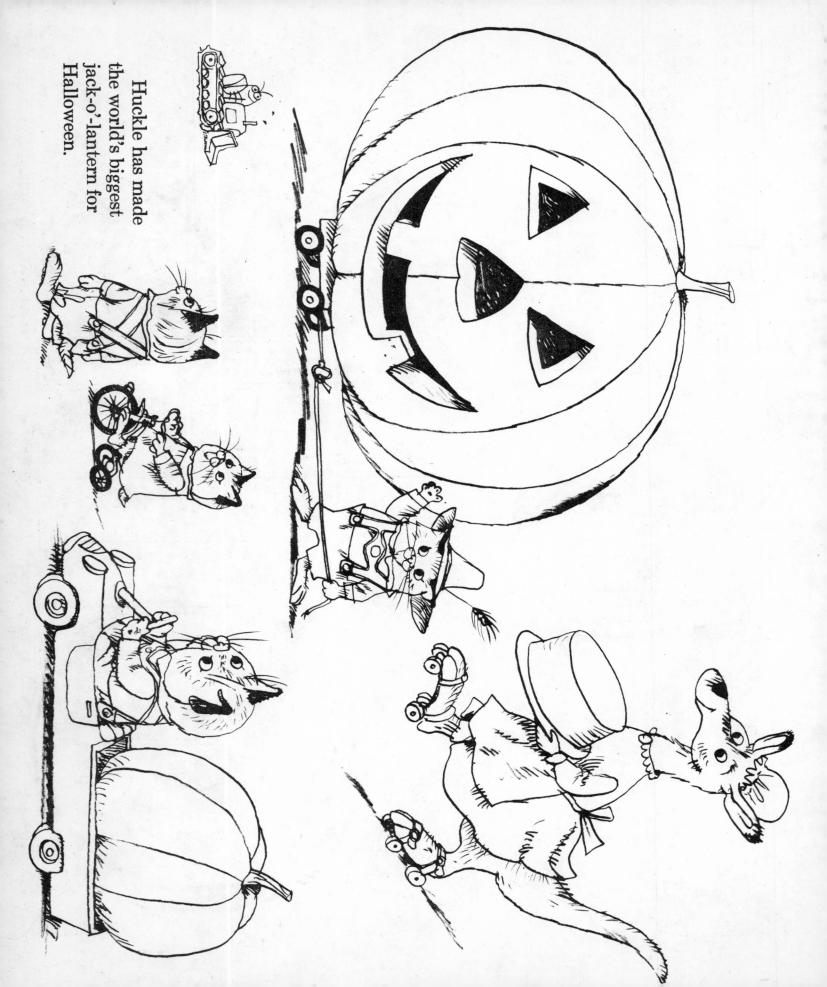

Huckle has made the world's biggest jack-o'-lantern for Halloween.

31 DAYS

OCTOBER

HALLOWEEN — OCT. 31

SUNDAY	MONDAY	TUESDAY	WEDNESDAY	THURSDAY	FRIDAY	SATURDAY

APPLES

apple cider

Oh, what a messy sight!

Who wants to play?

Time for a checkup. Say "Aah!"

Look at all the different drivers in Busy Town!

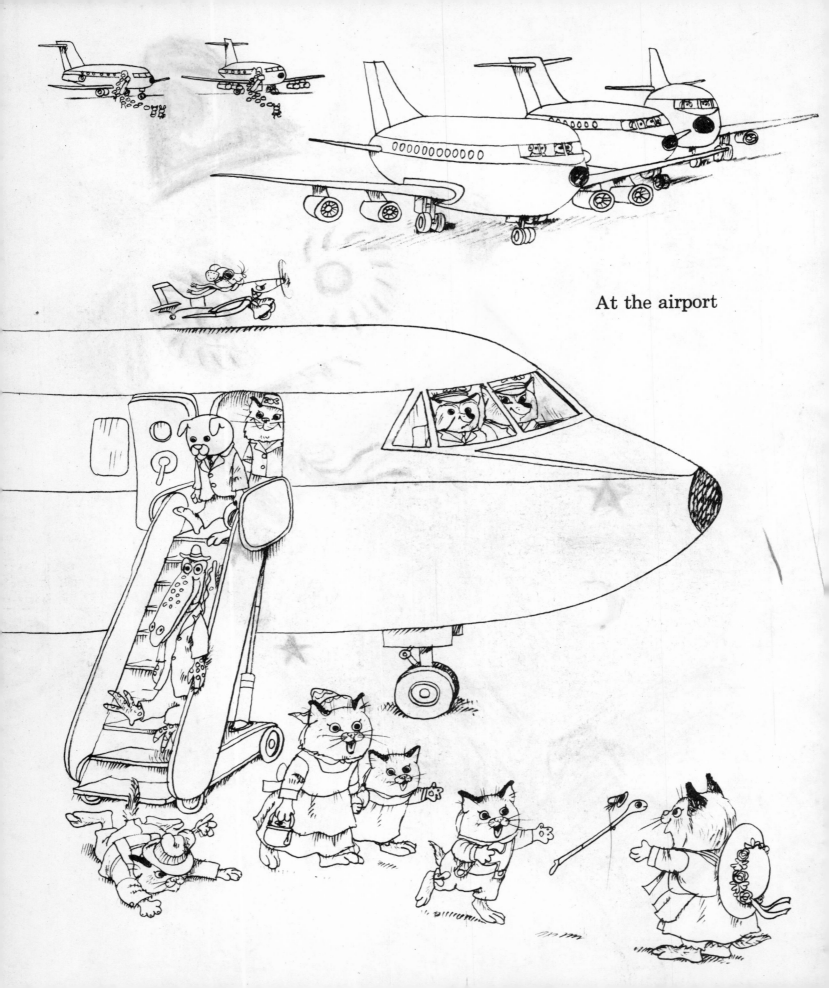

At the airport

A HALLOWEEN DECORATION

Color the witch on both sides of the page.
Cut out along the black outline.
Tape the witch to a window where everyone
can see it on Halloween.

Mr. Skunk is digging the
cellar for a new house.

Mr. Puffin and Mr. Parrot are going to a party. My, they look nice in their good clothes!

30 DAYS	NOVEMBER			THANKSGIVING DAY— 4th THURSDAY IN NOV.		
SUNDAY	MONDAY	TUESDAY	WEDNESDAY	THURSDAY	FRIDAY	SATURDAY

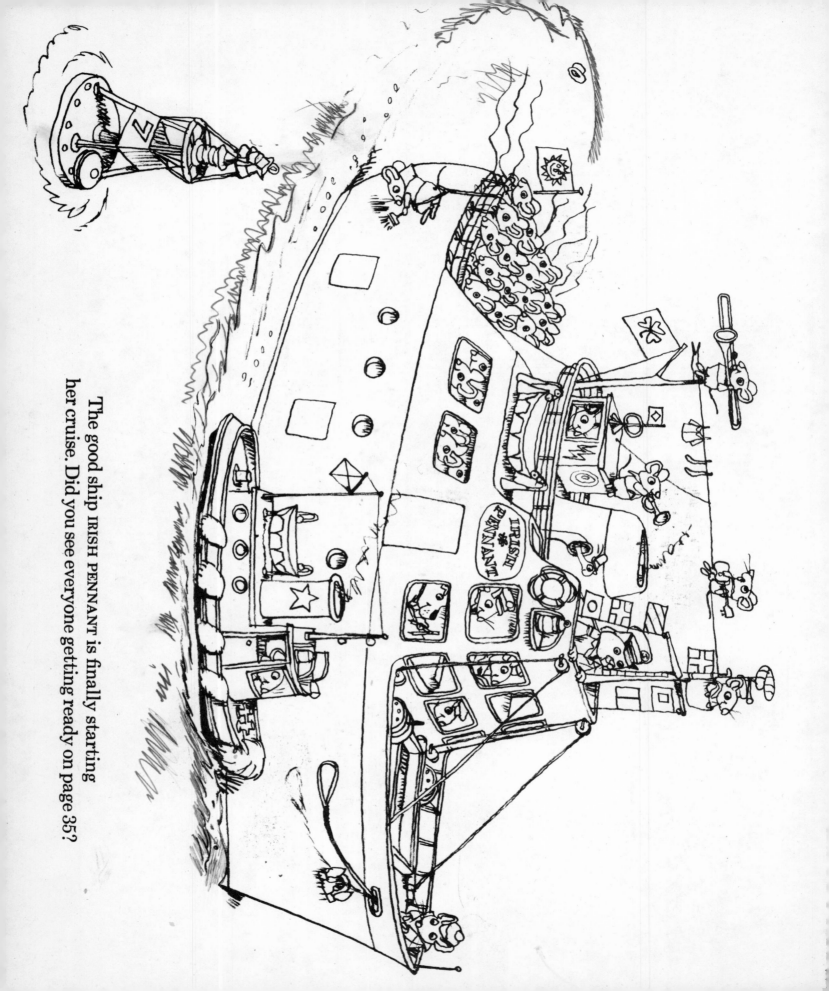

The good ship IRISH PENNANT is finally starting her cruise. Did you see everyone getting ready on page 35?

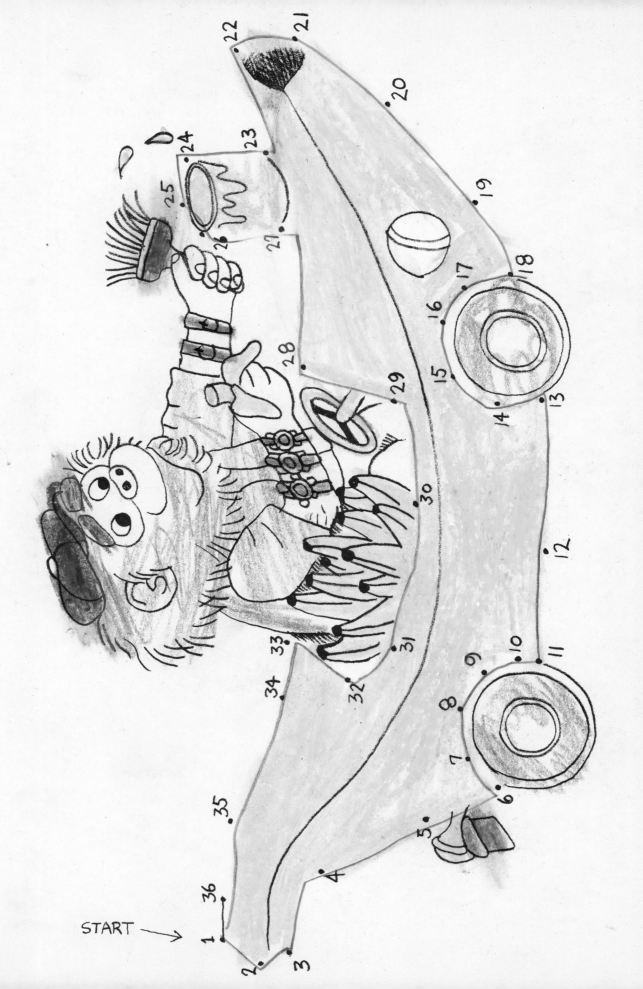

START →

What is Bananas Gorilla painting? Connect the dots and check your answer on page 6.

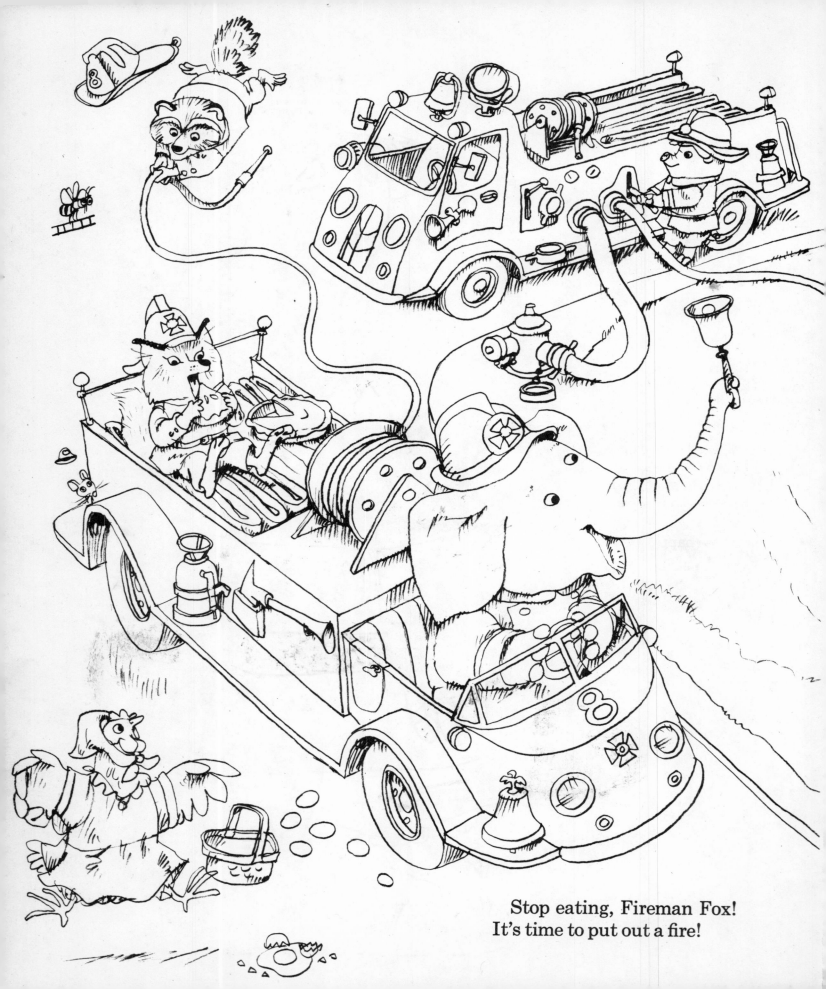

Stop eating, Fireman Fox!
It's time to put out a fire!

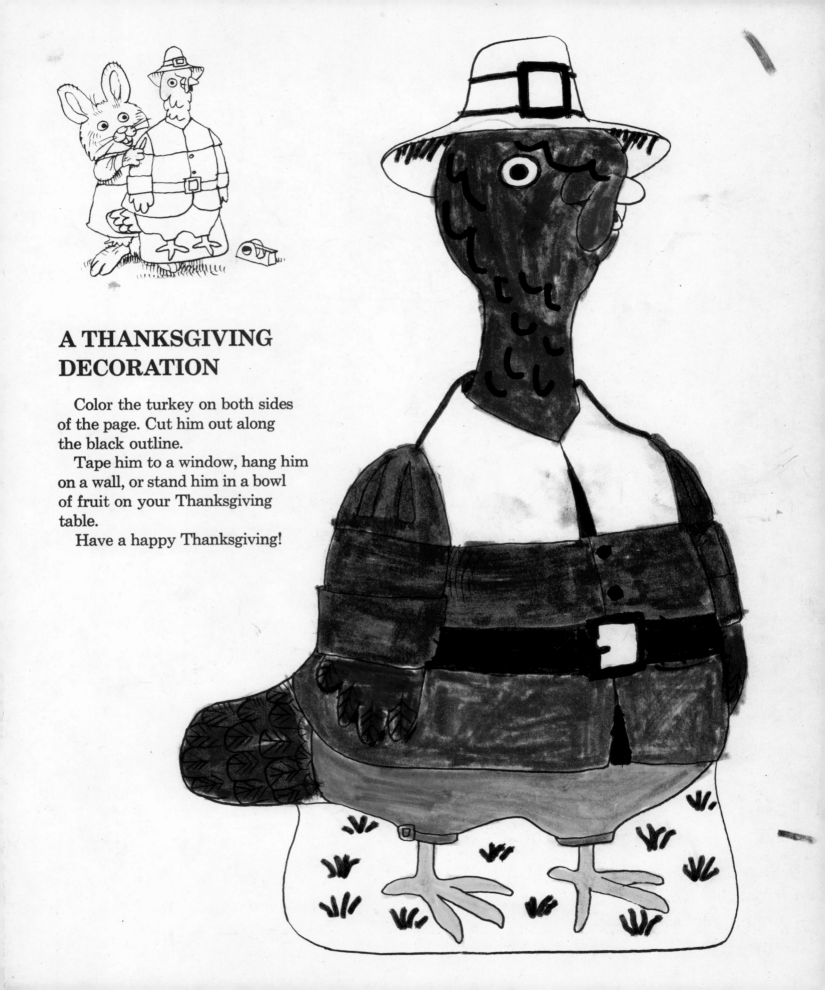

A THANKSGIVING DECORATION

Color the turkey on both sides of the page. Cut him out along the black outline.

Tape him to a window, hang him on a wall, or stand him in a bowl of fruit on your Thanksgiving table.

Have a happy Thanksgiving!

Oh-oh! Guess what's going to happen next!

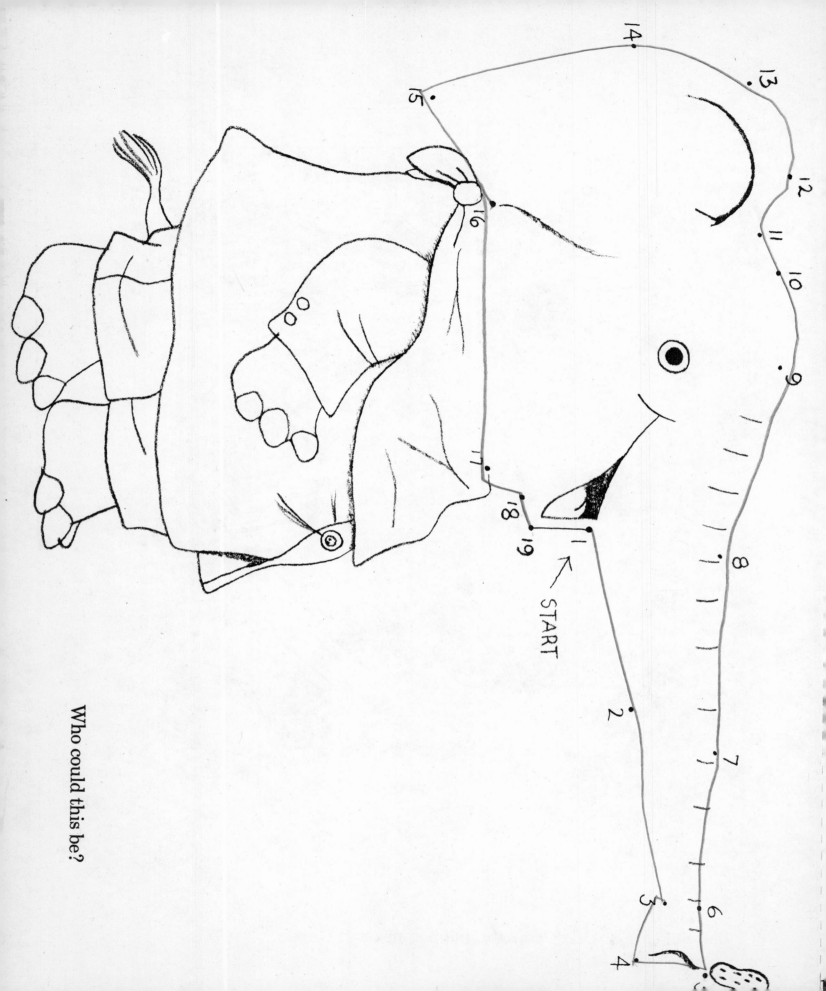

Who could this be?

· SUPERMARKET ·
MAKE ALL DELIVERIES AT THIS DOOR

CAFÉ OLÉ

BOOTS THE SHOEMAKER

GAR AND BAGE
·
SANITATION ENGINEERS

MADAME OVERALL'S
PARTY SHOP
BOOKS · FAVORS

BOOKS

Look both ways before
you cross the street
in Busy Town!

ICE CREAM

The children stand around
the Christmas tree singing
Christmas carols.
    Color the children and the
tree. You can sing, too!

31 DAYS	DECEMBER					CHRISTMAS DAY — DECEMBER 25
SUNDAY	MONDAY	TUESDAY	WEDNESDAY	THURSDAY	FRIDAY	SATURDAY

A quiet corner in Busy Town

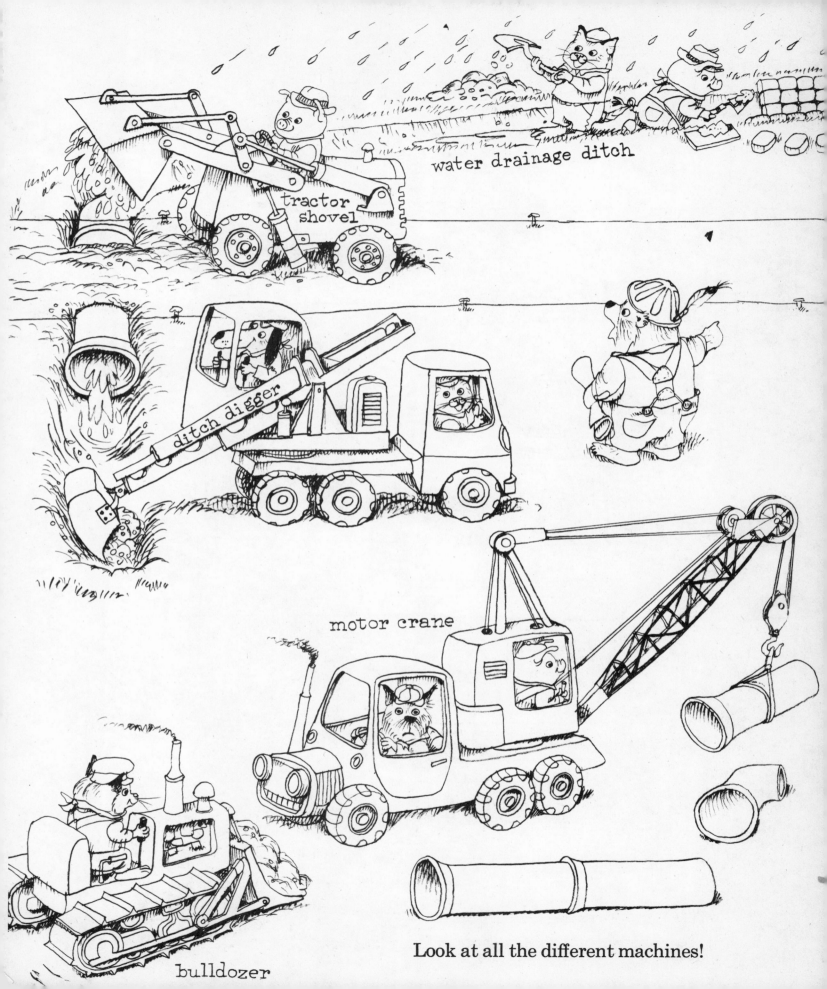

water drainage ditch

tractor shovel

ditch digger

motor crane

bulldozer

Look at all the different machines!

COLOR PRACTICE

Can you make all these objects the right color?

Red
apple
strawberry
fire engine
heart
the inside of a watermelon

Yellow
daffodil
banana
corn
lemon
cheese
bell

Green
peas
leaf
blades of grass
bug
clover leaf
lettuce
pine tree
the outside of a watermelon

BUGDOZER

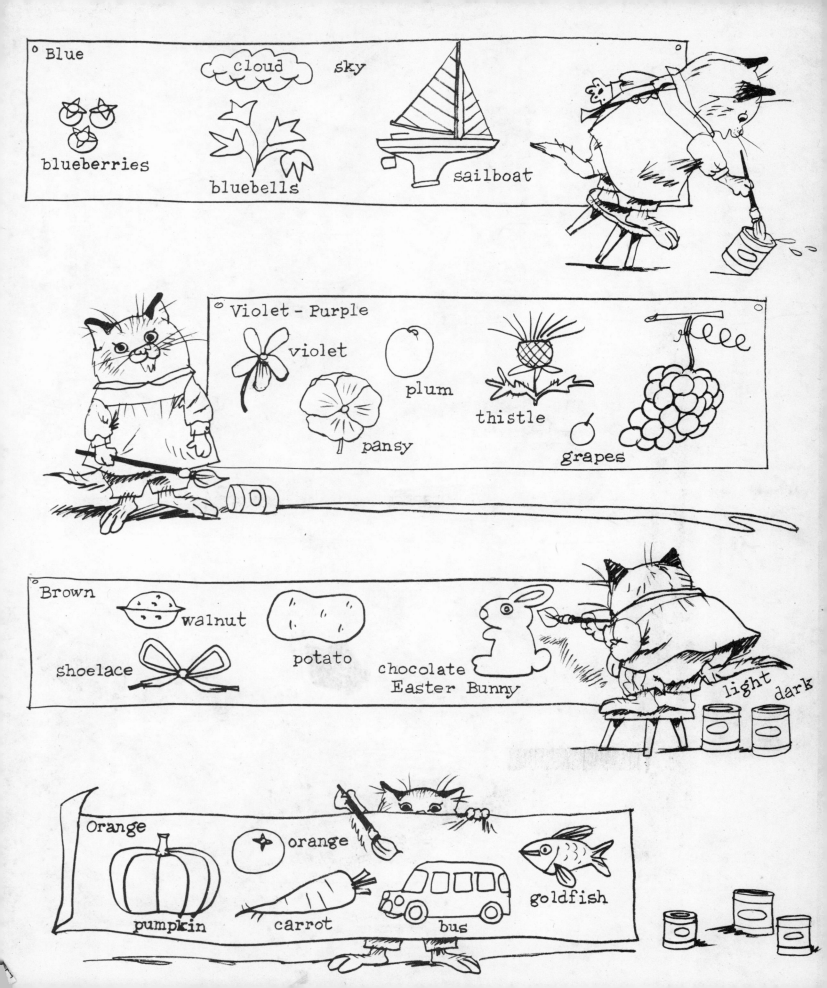

Blue

cloud   sky

blueberries

bluebells

sailboat

Violet - Purple

violet

plum

thistle

pansy

grapes

Brown

walnut

shoelace   potato

chocolate
Easter Bunny

light   dark

Orange

orange

pumpkin   carrot   bus   goldfish

At work in the forest

BOATS

Christmas carolers in the snow.

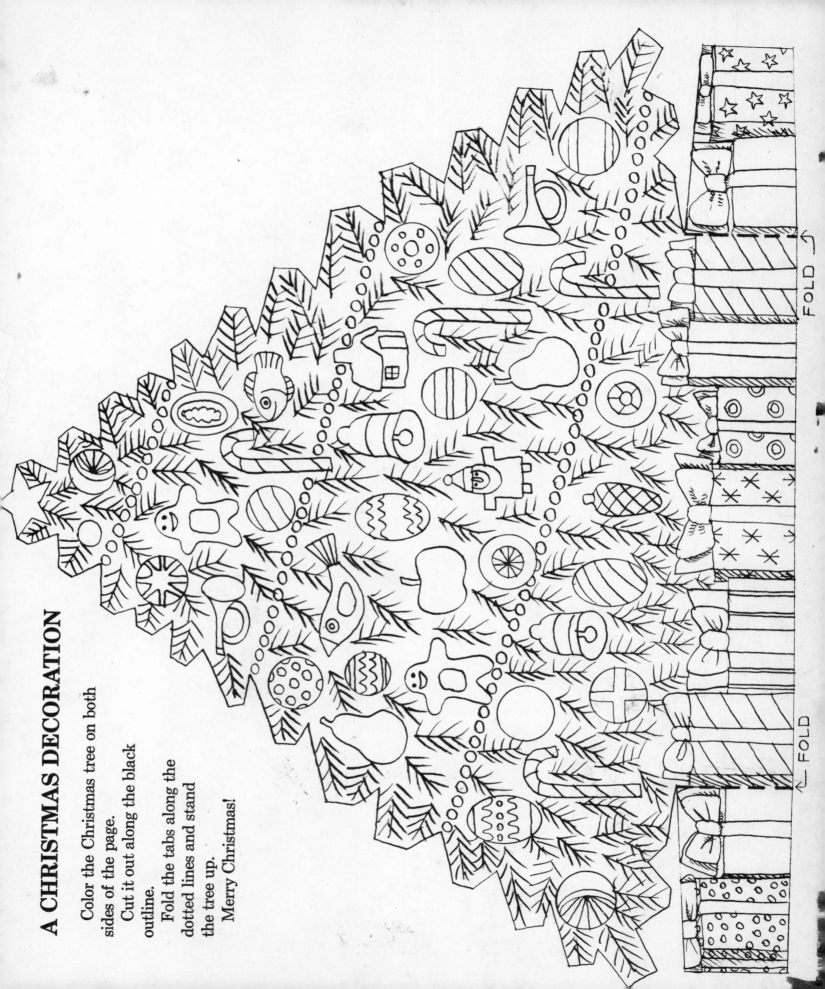

A CHRISTMAS DECORATION

Color the Christmas tree on both
sides of the page.
Cut it out along the black
outline.
Fold the tabs along the
dotted lines and stand
the tree up.
Merry Christmas!

FOLD

FOLD

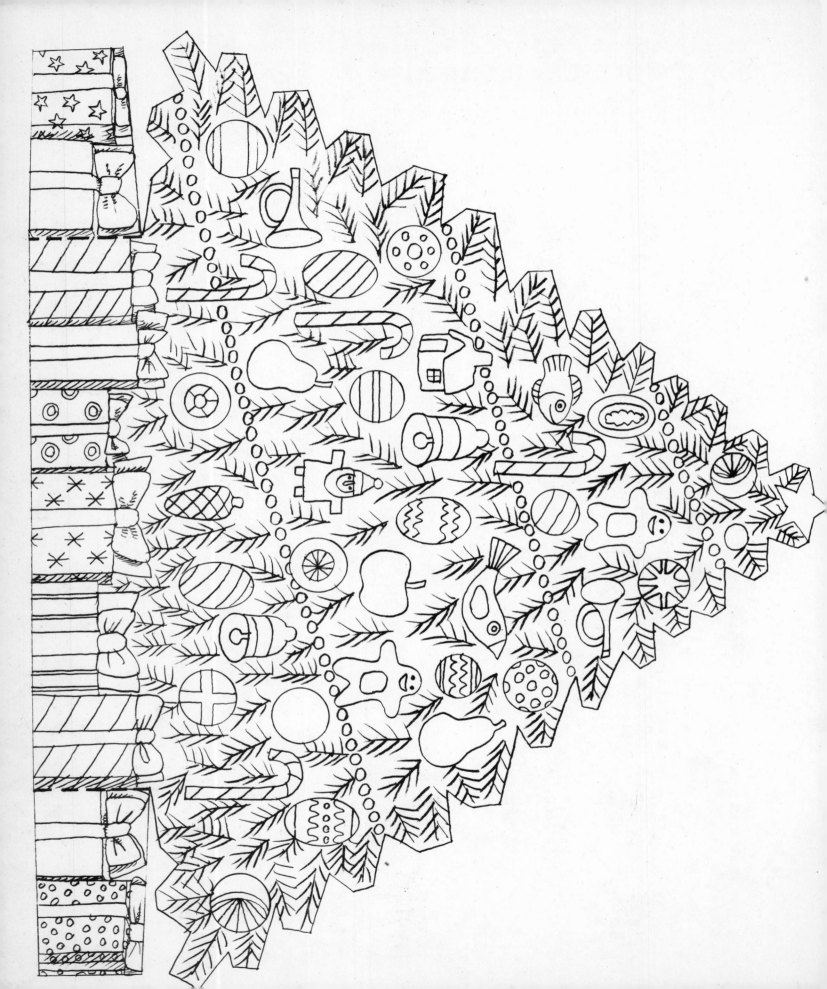

CHRISTMAS TREE ORNAMENTS

Here are 3 pages of ornaments for you to make.
Color them on both sides of the page. Cut them out along the black outlines.

With a pencil, gently punch a hole at the top of each ornament. Tie a string through each one.

Now you can hang the ornaments on your Christmas tree.

PUNCH HOLE
IN CIRCLE

Do your cutting on the other side of the page.

Directions for making
Christmas tree ornaments
are on page 171.

Do your cutting on
the other side of the page.

Directions for making
Christmas tree ornaments
are on page 171.

Do your cutting on
the other side of the page.